Business Groups and Strategic Coopetition

Business Groups and Strategic Coopetition sheds lights on the poorly recognised problem of intra-organisational relationships within business groups by adopting the coopetition lens. It brings together the strategic management (coopetition and performance) and international management perspectives (business groups and its role in the economy). It is a unique proposition as those two research streams, such as business groups and coopetition, are rarely assessed together. The coopetition, which is seen as the strategy of value creating in the rapidly changing environment, brings benefits, such as an increased innovation, cost reduction, access to resources, and improved competitive position that could be captured by business groups as well. However, the understanding of complex organisations, such as business group, and answering the question how to manage intra-level coopetition to gain better performance therein is still unclear. Therefore, the book aims to extend the knowledge in the field of internal relationships within business groups as well as the coopetition phenomenon. This book is written to meet needs of researchers, students, as well as managers and to present an integrated view on the coopetition within business groups.

Wioletta Mierzejewska is an associate professor at the Warsaw School of Economics in the Institute of Management, Poland.

Patryk Dziurski is an assistant professor at the Warsaw School of Economics in the Institute of Management, Poland.

Routledge Studies in Management, Organizations and Society

This series presents innovative work grounded in new realities, addressing issues crucial to an understanding of the contemporary world. This is the world of organized societies, where boundaries between formal and informal, public and private, local and global organizations have been displaced or have vanished, along with other nineteenth century dichotomies and oppositions. Management, apart from becoming a specialized profession for a growing number of people, is an everyday activity for most members of modern societies.

Similarly, at the level of enquiry, culture and technology, and literature and economics, can no longer be conceived as isolated intellectual fields; conventional canons and established mainstreams are contested. *Management, Organizations, and Society* addresses these contemporary dynamics of transformation in a manner that transcends disciplinary boundaries, with books that will appeal to researchers, students and practitioners alike.

Recent titles in this series include:

Business meets the Humanities
The Human Perspective in University-Industry Collaborations
Edited by Martina Skrubbeltrang Mahnke, Mikka Nielsen, Matilde Lykkebo Petersen and Lise Tjørring

Business Groups and Strategic Coopetition
Edited by Wioletta Mierzejewska and Patryk Dziurski

Flexible Human Resource Management and Vocational Behaviour
The Employability Market Orientation Model
Anna Pawłowska

Knowledge Communication in Global Organisations
Making Sense of Virtual Teams
Nils Braad Petersen

For more information about this series, please visit: https://www.routledge.com/Routledge-Studies-in-Genocide-and-Crimes-against-Humanity/book-series/RSGCH

Business Groups and Strategic Coopetition

Edited by
Wioletta Mierzejewska and
Patryk Dziurski

Routledge
Taylor & Francis Group
NEW YORK AND LONDON

First published 2023
by Routledge
605 Third Avenue, New York, NY 10158

and by Routledge
4 Park Square, Milton Park, Abingdon, Oxon, OX14 4RN

Routledge is an imprint of the Taylor & Francis Group, an informa business

Library of Congress Cataloging-in-Publication Data
Names: Mierzejewska, Wioletta, editor. | Dziurski, Patryk, 1989– editor.
Title: Business groups and strategic coopetition / edited by Wioletta Mierzejewska and Patryk Dziurski.
Description: 1 Edition. | New York, NY : Routledge, 2023. | Series: Routledge studies in management, organizations and society | Includes bibliographical references and index.
Identifiers: LCCN 2022031651 | ISBN 9781032349855 (hardback) | ISBN 9781032349879 (paperback) | ISBN 9781003324775 (ebook)
Subjects: LCSH: International business enterprises—Management. | Organizational behavior. | Strategic planning. | Competition.
Classification: LCC HD2755.5 .B8867 2023 | DDC 382.06/5—dc23/engg/20220916
LC record available at https://lccn.loc.gov/2022031651

This book is supported by a research grant from the National Science Centre under the project titled: Coopetition in Business Groups: Scale, Nature, Determinants, and Impact on Effectiveness [Koopetycja w grupach kapitałowych – skala, charakter, determinanty i wpływ na efektywność] (Grant No 2017/25/B/HS4/02448).

ISBN: 978-1-032-34985-5 (hbk)
ISBN: 978-1-032-34987-9 (pbk)
ISBN: 978-1-003-32477-5 (ebk)

DOI: 10.4324/9781003324775

Typeset in Bembo
by codeMantra

Contents

Contributors

Maria Aluchna
SGH Warsaw School of Economics
Warsaw, Poland

Maria Aluchna is the professor of management at the SGH Warsaw School of Economics, the head of the Department of Management Theory, and the chair of the Management Faculty Board (Poland). She specialises in corporate governance, strategic management, and corporate social responsibility. She teaches corporate governance case studies, responsible management, and strategic management at the undergraduate, graduate, and postgraduate levels. She is a member of the European Corporate Governance Institute, International Corporate Governance Society, Finance Watch, and European Academy of Management. She publishes in Poland and abroad and takes active part in international conferences.

Patryk Dziurski
SGH Warsaw School of Economics
Warsaw, Poland

Patryk Dziurski is the assistant professor at the SGH Warsaw School of Economics in the Institute of Management (Poland). He does quantitative and qualitative research in strategic management, innovation and open innovation, marketing, as well as cultural and creative industries. He has many years of experience as a lecturer at the undergraduate, graduate, and postgraduate levels in the field of strategic management, innovation, and marketing. He is the author of many publications in management and member of the European Academy of Management and the Academy of International Business.

Rumiana Górska
SGH Warsaw School of Economics
Warsaw, Poland

Rumiana Górska is the assistant professor at the SGH Warsaw School of Economics in the Institute of Econometrics (Poland). She teaches statistics, econometrics, econometric methods, time series econometrics, financial mathematics, and operations research. She conducts training for employees of the National Bank of Poland and the Ministry of Finance of the Republic of Bulgaria, and she cooperated with Deloitte Polska, PKP PLK, and Avon Cosmetics.

Mirosław Jarosiński
SGH Warsaw School of Economics
Warsaw, Poland

Mirosław Jarosiński is the associate professor at the SGH Warsaw School of Economics and the head of the Department of International Management (Poland). He is also the CEMS Academic Director at SGH. He is the founder of the master's programme in International Business at SGH, and he was its director in years 2006–2011. He teaches master's in International Business at SGH and CEMS master's in International Management. His research focuses on internationalisation processes of firms with a special attention to international new ventures and similar types of entrepreneurial ventures operating internationally. He is a member of IEDF, AIELF, EIBA, and AIB (since July 2016 a board member of AIB-CEE Chapter).

Mateusz Juchniewicz
SGH Warsaw School of Economics
Warsaw, Poland

Mateusz Juchniewicz is the associate professor at the SGH Warsaw School of Economics and the head of the Department of Project Management (Poland). He is a lecturer at the undergraduate, graduate, and postgraduate levels and manager and participant of scientific, consulting, and training projects. He cooperates with both public and private sectors. He specialises in project management maturity, risk management in projects, and projects in a multicultural environment. He is the author of several dozen publications in the field of management, certified project manager in the field of project management, and member of Project Management Institute and International Project Management Association.

Anna Krejner-Nowecka
SGH Warsaw School of Economics
Warsaw, Poland

Anna Krejner-Nowecka is the assistant professor at the SGH Warsaw School of Economics in the Institute of Management (Poland). She specialises in international human resource management, organisational behaviour, diversity management, and cultural differences in business as well as in corporate restructuring and outsourcing. She teaches at bachelor, master, and post-graduate levels. She is the author of articles and papers for conferences at the national as well as international levels and member of Academy of International Business and the Organization and Management Committee of the Polish Academy of Sciences.

Wioletta Mierzejewska
SGH Warsaw School of Economics
Warsaw, Poland

Wioletta Mierzejewska is the associate professor at the SGH Warsaw School of Economics and the vice-director of the Institute of Management (Poland). She specialises in strategic management, innovation, business groups, and structural transformations of enterprises. She is the author of numerous studies and papers on these issues. She has many years of experience in business projects and as a lecturer at the undergraduate, graduate, and postgraduate levels in the field of strategic management and organisational design. She is a member of the Academy of International Business, the European Academy of Management, the Program Council of the European Foundation for Entrepreneurship Development, and the Management Faculty Board at SGH Warsaw School of Economics.

Agnieszka Sopińska
SGH Warsaw School of Economics
Warsaw, Poland

Agnieszka Sopińska is the professor at the SGH Warsaw School of Economics in the Institute of Management (Poland) and member of the Organization and Management Committee of the Polish Academy of Sciences. She specialises in strategic management, innovation management, and knowledge management. She has many years of experience as a lecturer at the undergraduate, graduate, and postgraduate levels in the field of strategic management and innovation management. She is the author or co-author of more than 160 publications on management. She actively cooperates with management consulting firms as well as training companies.

Piotr Wachowiak
SGH Warsaw School of Economics
Warsaw, Poland

Piotr Wachowiak is the rector of the SGH Warsaw School of Economics, director of the Institute of Management (Poland), vice-president of the Organization and Management Committee of the Polish Academy of Sciences, chairman of the Entrepreneurship Council, an advisory body for the President of the Republic of Poland, and a member of the

CSR working group at the Ministry of Investment and Development. He specialises in human resource management, negotiations, corporate social responsibility, measuring enterprises' intellectual capital and knowledge management in enterprises, as well as innovation. He e is the author or co-author of many publications in management.

Figures

Tables

Introduction

Wioletta Mierzejewska and Patryk Dziurski

Coopetition, defined as the interplay between cooperation and competition that emerges simultaneously among different parties, has gained considerable attention in the management literature. It is one of the key strategies in a turbulent environment as coopetition helps organisations to survive and grow with the changing conditions of competition, emergence of hyper-competition, rapid technological progress, and increasing globalisation. This kind of relationship can be found in different industries, such as automotive, electronics, and pharmaceutical, in which standalone firms simultaneously cooperate in the development of new technologies and/or products and compete in sales to gain leading position in the global market. Coopetition is, therefore, seen as a strategy of value building in a rapidly changing environment. Benefits of cooperation with competitors are, among others, increased innovation, cost reduction, access to resources, and improved competitive position.

Coopetition is most often studied at the inter-organisational (inter-firm) level between legally and economically independent entities. It could be two (dyadic coopetition), three (triadic coopetition), or more standalone organisations (network coopetition). This type of coopetition is well examined. However, previous studies on coopetition proved that simultaneous cooperation and competition can be found also within complex organisations. This type of coopetition is called intra-organisational (intra-firm), and some researchers argue that it has been still insufficiently recognised (Bendig et al., 2018; Crick, 2019; Chen et al., 2020) and thus it is a promising and important research area (Becker-Ritterspach & Dörrenbächer, 2011; Gernsheimer et al., 2021).

The book focuses on the intra-organisational perspective and analyses coopetition within complex organisations that business groups are. Business groups are collections of legally independent entities bound by ownership ties with one centre of power and control. They are common in various economies, both developed and developing. The number of business groups has been increasing, and they have become important players in the regional and global economy. However, each region has its own specificity of business groups related to the type, main industries, size, and organisational design. Despite regional differences, relations between

DOI: 10.4324/9781003324775-1

units forming all business groups are mainly cooperative, because they strive to achieve common goals. Cooperation inside business groups concerns knowledge transfer, operations, marketing, HR management, financing, and other functions. However, the long life cycle of a business group leads to competitive behaviour among subsidiaries. They compete for the limited resources of the parent company, position within a business group, power, and external and internal clients, or due to the domain overlap. Coopetition within a business group can be emergent in nature or incentivised by the parent company to achieve better organisational performance. It should be highlighted that coopetition within business groups differs from inter-organisational and network coopetition, because subsidiaries are not fully independent in making decisions and with strategic choices. This is a type of intra-organisational coopetition that is poorly recognised and understood.

The main goal of the book is to shed some light and understanding on inter-subsidiary coopetition relations. Thus, the book is organised into ten chapters, which answer the following questions:

- Is coopetition a frequent relation within business groups and what are its features?
- What kind of tensions are linked with intra-group coopetition and how can managers overcome them?
- What are the main internal and external drivers of coopetition within business groups?
- What is the relationship between coopetition within business groups and corporate governance, international scale of operations, and subsidiaries' resource endowment?
- Are there any differences in coopetition in high-, medium-, and low-tech industries?
- What are the financial outcomes of coopetition within business groups?
- How to manage coopetition within business groups?

The book presents research carried on 121 Polish business groups between 2018 and 2020. The research sample consists of business groups listed on the Warsaw Stock Exchange (WSE) as they are obliged to publish reliable data and some additional information can also be acquired. In October 2018, after analysis of published documents of all companies listed on the WSE Main Market, 277 business groups (excluding financial ones) were identified. In the next stage, 121 business groups were randomly selected from the total amount of identified business groups. All data for further analysis were collected via surveys with top managers of parent companies (Tsai, 2002). Previous studies on the intra-organisational coopetition explore narrow and specific issues related to coopetition, mostly from a subsidiary's perspective (Luo, 2005; Tippmann et al., 2018). This study implements a helicopter perspective of the whole business group represented by the parent company as it plays a significant role in a business group, coordinates cooperation between subsidiaries, as well as might stimulate internal competition. Therefore, surveys were conducted with senior managers from parent companies as it allows to gather information about strategic choices and behaviours of the whole business group. It enables also to assess different issues related to coopetition across the whole business group and provides additional insights into intra-organisational coopetition compared to previous studies.

Interviews with top managers were conducted using a standardised questionnaire with the use of computer-assisted telephone interviewing (CATI method). Based on the perception of top managers, features of coopetition within business groups were identified. Additional data related to the industry, employment, geographical scope of operations, financial performance, and shareholders were acquired from the Amadeus database and financial statements published by business groups.

Business groups in the study are moderately differentiated. The geographical scope of operations ranges from national (25.6%), through Central and Eastern Europe (7.4%) and European Economic Area (33.9%), to global (25.6%). According to the NACE Rev. 2 (NACE is a statistical classification of economic activities in the European Community), most of business groups in the sample represent manufacturing (38.8%), wholesale and retail trade, repair of motor vehicles and motorcycles (14.9%), and construction (12.4%). An analysis of business groups' size by employment reveals that the sample is dominated by large entities with more than 250 employees (61.2%). Only 15.7% of business groups employ between 51 and 250 employees and 8.3% of business groups are small corporations with fewer than 50 employees. Domestic shareholders dominate in the sample (81.0%) and only 17.4% of business groups have foreign major shareholder. Shareholder is mainly individual (44.6%) or industry shareholder (32.2%).

The research conducted provides insights into the phenomenon of intra-organisational coopetition enabling to better understand the complex nature of relations between subsidiaries in a business group. The book is organised into ten chapters that discuss issues related to coopetition within business groups. The first chapter discusses the concept of a business group. It also elaborates the emergence of business groups, their different classifications, and importance on the Polish market. The second chapter presents the essence of coopetition and its various patterns within business groups. The next chapter is devoted to tensions and behavioural aspects of coopetition. The fourth chapter discusses then internal and external factors of coopetition within business groups. The fifth chapter elaborates the relationship between coopetition within business groups and subsidiaries' resource endowment, while the sixth chapter focuses on the coopetition within international business groups. The next chapter refers to the coopetition within business groups and corporate governance, which is followed by the chapter that concentrates on differences in coopetition within business groups that operate in high-, medium-, and low-tech industries. The ninth chapter assesses the relationship between financial outcomes of business groups and coopetition therein. The last chapter includes conclusions and guidelines of how to manage coopetition within business groups.

The research conducted reduces the emerging research gap on simultaneous cooperation and competition between entities within business groups. Authors hope that the book, which shows the holistic phenomenon of coopetition within business groups, is useful for both scholars and managers. The book was also written with the aim to inspire and encourage further studies to deepen understanding of the concept of business groups and coopetition with emphasis on intra-organisational level relations.

References

Becker-Ritterspach, F. & Dörrenbächer, C. (2011). An organizational politics perspective on intra-firm competition in multinational corporations. *Management International Review*, 51(4), 533–559.

Bendig, D., Enke, S., Thieme, N. & Brettel, M. (2018). Performance implications of cross-functional coopetition in new product development: The mediating role of organizational learning. *Industrial Marketing Management*, 73, 137–153.

Chen, M., Tang, T.Y., Wu, S. & Wang, F. (2020). The double-edged sword of coopetition: Differential effects of cross-functional coopetition on product and service innovations. *Journal of Business & Industrial Marketing*, 36(2), 191–202.

Crick, J.M. (2019). The dark side of coopetition: When collaborating with competitors is harmful for company performance. *Journal of Business & Industrial Marketing*, 35(2), 318–337.

Gernsheimer, O., Kanbach, D.K. & Gast, J. (2021). Coopetition research: A systematic literature review on recent accomplishments and trajectories. *Industrial Marketing Management*, 96, 113–134.

Luo, Y. (2005). Toward coopetition within a multinational enterprise: A perspective from foreign subsidiaries. *Journal of World Business*, 40(1), 71–90.

Tippmann, E., Scott, P.S., Reilly, M. & O'Brien, D. (2018). Subsidiary coopetition competence: Navigating subsidiary evolution in the multinational corporation. *Journal of World Business*, 53(4), 540–554.

Tsai, W. (2002). Social structure of "coopetition" within a multiunit organization: Coordination, competition, and intraorganizational knowledge sharing. *Organization Science*, 13(2), 179–190.

1 The Essence of Business Groups

Wioletta Mierzejewska and Piotr Wachowiak

Introduction

The first business groups were established at the beginning of the 19th century in Europe (Belgium, England, Switzerland, and Germany) and in the mid-19th century in the United States. The intense business concentration trend, taking place in the global economy from the mid-20th century, has made a business group a commonly used organisational model around the world. The importance of business groups in the global economy has been significant and constantly growing. Business groups are ubiquitous in many countries as they can be found in both developed and developing economies. Japan's *keiretsus* and *zaibatsu*, South Korea's *chaebols*, Latin America's *grupos economicos*, Hong Kong's *hongs*, India's *business houses*, Taiwan's *guanxiqiye*, Russia's *oligarchs*, and China's *qiye jitu* are emblematic for national economic systems (Carney et al., 2011). They differ in terms of organisation, strategy, and reasons of emergence but share some similarities such as legal independence of subsidiaries, range of economic and social ties, and complex coordination mechanisms. Business group is a relevant form of organisation for small and large entities with different scale of operations (Iacobucci & Rosa, 2005). Some business groups were set up relatively recently, others exist for a long time (Cuervo-Cazurra, 2018). This diversity makes business groups an interesting and important research area.

The aim of the chapter is to shed lights on the phenomenon of business groups, especially those operating in Poland, by focusing on four important issues. The first one refers to the definition of a business group. It is difficult to define it due to different approaches existing in the literature. The second issue concerns reasons that business groups emerged, for which there is no one-fits-all explanation. The chapter discusses some main approaches behind the creation of business groups. The third issue focuses on the variety of business groups in the economy. Various classifications of a business group allow for a better understanding of its specificity but also show its complexity and diversity. Finally, as business groups differ depending on their geographical origin, emphasis is put on the specificity of business groups operating in Poland.

DOI: 10.4324/9781003324775-2

Definition of a Business Group

The growth of the global economy has resulted in the emergence of various types of complex organisations, such as business groups that are kind of collection of companies. They should be distinguished from i.e. geographical networks, clusters, investment funds, business networks, strategic networks, or alliances. All those organisations lack some features that are related to business groups, despite the abundance and variety of business group definitions (Cuervo-Cazurra, 2018). Putting it simple, a business group is understood as a set of firms having a common owner (Almeida et al., 2011), or in other words, a set of subsidiaries owned by the parent company (Iacobucci & Rosa, 2005). Wider definitions indicate that a business group is a set of legally independent entities connected by economic (ownership, financial, commercial) and social (family, kinship, friendship) ties (Chung, 2001; Yiu et al., 2005), or according to a different interpretation by formal and informal ties (Khanna & Rivkin, 2001; Carney et al., 2011). Encarnation (1989) points out on the example of Indian business houses that "strong social ties of family, caste, religion, language, ethnicity and region reinforced financial and organisational linkages" (1989: 45). Those numerous and overlapping ties bid together affiliated firms and enable them to undertake coordinated actions. Affiliated firms exchange resources and information, share a brand name, group together resources to invest new ventures, draw on a common labour pool, and rely on each other for financing (Khanna & Rivkin, 2001; Fisman & Khanna, 2004). Business groups implement also complex coordination mechanisms, such as multiple and reciprocated equity, debt, and commercial ties as well as kinship affiliation between top managers (Carney et al., 2011). Those features make business groups better at dealing with failures on financial, labour, and product markets (Fisman & Khanna, 2004). Thus, they are often found in emerging or developing economies. Business groups are present also in all developed economies, although in some of them (e.g. the United States) legislation limited their growth (Colpan & Hikino, 2018; Cuervo-Cazurra, 2018).

Numerous definitions draw attention to different features of a business group, for example, single common administrative and financial control (Chang & Hong, 2002), undertaking joint coordinated actions (Khanna & Rivkin, 2001), stable strategic relationships (Cuervo-Cazurra, 2006), equity cross-ownership and common board membership (Fisman & Khanna, 2004), common strategic and ownership control (Cuervo-Cazurra, 2018), and operating together in a coherent manner (Chung, 2001). Other definitions link a business group to family ownership (Chang & Hong, 2002), although some other definitions point to other types of ownership structure (Cuervo-Cazurra, 2006). Interestingly, some definitions point to diversification as a feature of a business group too (Khanna & Palepu, 2000; Fisman & Khanna, 2004; Cuervo-Cazurra, 2018).

Business groups are often defined from the perspective of resource-based view and network approach. Researchers indicate that business groups are a kind of platform enabling resource sharing (Chang & Hong, 2002; Hsieh et al., 2010). Business groups possess an inimitable capability to combine domestic and foreign resources allowing cost-effective and quick entry to new industries (Guillen, 2000). At the same time, business groups are a specific type of inter-organisational network (Khanna & Rivkin, 2006; Popli et al., 2017) with stable equity connections between network nodes. Some researchers clearly indicate that business groups have similar features to network organisations (Ćwik, 2013; Dmowska & Mikucka-Kowalczyk, 2019). One can observe vertical disintegration, an entity acting as a broker, repeatability of resource flows, or the occurrence of intensive information exchange. Thus, business groups are a well-structured network with clear boundaries and clear architecture. Researchers argue that business groups act as an internal network for integration and exchange of knowledge, experience, and resources between affiliated firms. However, not all affiliates have an equal position within the network, and those bound with family ties to the core company can be seen as the most important (Hsieh et al., 2010).

Sociology and economics-based approaches are often implemented for identifying the essence of a business group (Cuervo-Cazurra, 2006; Aluchna, 2010). The first approach is much broader. Business groups are distinguished based on both formal and informal links of varying intensity (Granovetter, 1995). In this approach, great importance is attached to family and social ties linking legally independent entities (Luo & Chung, 2005) and to relations of trust from a similar ethnic or commercial origin (Leff, 1978). The second approach, economics-based, is much narrower, which allows to distinguish business groups from other network structures (supplier, distribution, strategic such as technology alliances or research consortia, but also geographical networks). In this approach, definitions focus on the issues of diversification, administrative and financial control, equity cross-ownership, and performance aspects of business groups (Cuervo-Cazurra, 2006; Aluchna, 2010). Thus, business groups are perceived as a coherent organisation model with the holding (parent) company at the top that owns, and controls operating units organised as subsidiaries and affiliates through equity ties and other, such as interlocking of directorates, budget allocation, and intra-group transactions (Colpan & Hikino, 2010).

The chapter and the whole book adopt the economics-based approach definition of a business group as it best suits the specificity of business groups operating in Poland. Therefore, business groups are defined as a set of legally independent entities under common management, cooperating in the implementation of common goals and connected by permanent ownership (equity) ties and, additionally, other ties. Those additional ties include both commercial ties and various types of social ties, reflecting the network nature of a business group. It is, therefore, assumed that criteria necessary to distinguish business groups refer to a common goal, number of subsidiaries (at least two), and existence of formal ties between entities, including ownership ties (Aluchna, 2010).

Emergence of Business Groups

There are various reasons for a business group to emerge across the world meaning that there is no generally applicable theory explaining the formation of a business group. Previous studies focused on three basic explanations: market imperfection (institutional void), cultural heritage (relational perspective), and political economy. Those perspectives should be supplemented by the agency theory that sheds lights on business groups as well.

The institutional void theory argues that business groups exist due to market imperfections that manifest themselves through inefficient markets for labour, capital, technology, information asymmetry, weak corporate governance and control, lack of some financial institutions, and ineffective legal infrastructure (Leff, 1978; Khanna & Palepu, 1997; Yiu et al., 2007; Carney et al., 2011). Markets in emerging economies are often perceived as underdeveloped, which increases the probability of opportunistic behaviour. The consequence of market imperfection is high transaction costs (Khanna & Rivkin, 2001, 2006). The formation of a business group enables to create internal markets and overcome problems through internalisation of market transactions (Zhang et al., 2016). Internal markets within business groups enable better allocation and exchange of various types of assets, services, and goods (Yiu et al., 2007). Some scholars focus primarily on underdeveloped financial markets that cause business problems and block growth of standalone firms. Business groups create an internal capital market to secure financial needs of affiliated firms and allow for more effective allocation and use of resources (Gonenc & Hermes, 2008). Funds are allocated into projects with higher efficiency and better prospectus (Almeida et al., 2015). Business groups may also alleviate failures in labour, product, and technology markets (Carney et al., 2011; Sutherland & Lutao, 2015). Different studies prove the positive effects of business group affiliation and perceive them as value-enhancing organisations (Khanna & Rivkin, 2001; Chang & Hong, 2002). However, some researchers are more critical to the market imperfection argument and point out that business groups exist also in developed economies with no institutional deficits (Maman, 2002; Carney et al., 2011).

Another research stream explaining the existence of business groups has its roots in the sociology (Granovetter, 1984) and cultural background of organisations (Chung, 2001). Relational perspectives suggest that the main determinant of the existence of a business group is not always economic rationale. It focuses on solidarity norms, codes of behaviour, and cultural heritage. This stream of research also perceives business groups as value-enhancing organisations (Carney et al., 2011). It is a commonly used approach to explain family-business groups' emergence. Chung (2001) gives the example of Chinese business groups, in which entrepreneurs establish several separate firms instead of a single hierarchy to give male descendants a share. This approach is based on the patrimonial concept of authority and loyalty of other family members (Guillen, 2000). However, cultural determinism explains only similarities but not differences in business groups' emergence (Maman, 2002) and depends highly on the institutional environment in which organisations are embedded (Chung, 2001). Simultaneously, it gives an insight into business group evolution shaped by cultural heritage in different geographical regions (Yiu et al., 2007).

The third research stream is grounded in the political economy of societies and suggests that emergence of a business group depends on relations between state and society (Maman, 2002). Business groups exist because government establishes them into strategic industries or encourages entrepreneurs to set up them (Guillen, 2000; Yiu et al., 2007; Singh & Gaur, 2009). It could be tax incentives that encourage the creation of new business groups or the market deregulation to attract new investments and set up new entities (Hsieh et al., 2010). The creation of business groups is supported by governments as it helps them implement ambitious development plans. Business groups provide employment, and export their products and services, and they are strongly influential and perceived as an efficient information channel for influencing the private economy (Maman, 2002). Collin (1998) argues that two business groups in Sweden exist due to the government support. From this perspective, business groups are meant to promote state control and accelerate industrial development (Yiu et al., 2007).

The agency theory gives a different approach than previous perspectives of a business group establishment and functioning. It exposes the dark sides of a business group, which is perceived as a collection of agency relationships between controlling and minority shareholders (Yiu et al., 2007). The controlling shareholder (often family) through a unique ownership structure, called "pyramid ownership", controls many businesses with limited capital investments. This ownership structure enables them to expropriate the minority shareholders' wealth by "tunnelling" resources i.e. transfer profits to the core firm with family equity ownership predominance (Yiu et al., 2007; Carney et al., 2011). From this perspective, business groups are perceived as a kind of device through which rent goes to families controlling the group with detrimental effect on other minority shareholders. Thus, the main reason of business group emergence and existence is financial benefit for the main shareholder (Claessens et al., 2002; Carney et al., 2011).

Approaches presented to the business group formation are the basic ones. There are also many other explanations of the emergence and existence of business groups. Some researchers argue that an important perspective to the formation and growth of business groups is the entrepreneurship process, which implies that business groups are dynamic outcomes of growth processes often linked with the diversification (Iacobucci & Rosa, 2005). The formation of a business group is also analysed from the resource-based perspective. Business groups are created if political and economic conditions allow them to acquire and maintain the capability of combining foreign and domestic resources (Guillen, 2000) that are applicable to different industries. Those resources sustain a competitive advantage of a business group and are needed for further expansion. Other factors of a business group existence are economies of scale and scope, risk reduction, international political and economic development, political influence, accumulation of power, and so on (Maman, 2002; Schneider, 2009; Barbero & Puig, 2016).

In Poland, business groups emerged with the economic transformation in the early 1990s. Organisational and ownership changes of firms drove business groups' intensive development. Business groups emerged as a response to the dynamic change of the environment as well as freedom to make economic decisions (Romanowska, 1998). There were few paths of forming business groups. Some of them were established because of the transformation of multi-plant state-owned enterprises. Part of business groups followed privatisation to gain a strategic investor, and some have remained as a state-owned. Another path of business groups emergence in the early 1990s was related to the General Privatisation Programme, which enabled to form 15 National Investment Funds (NIF) based on several hundred privatised state-owned enterprises. NIF acted as business groups, but only a few managed to survive, while the rest went bankrupt. At the beginning of the economic transformation, business groups were also formed around banks. The process of bank consolidation by taking over weak and merging strong ones was accompanied by entering new activities. This resulted in the emergence of large financial business groups that also operated in related industries (Romanowska, 1998). Simultaneously to those paths of business groups' emergence, many new organisations appeared after the economic transformation. Those were completely different business groups, with a private investor, often a family, without the burden of privatised state-owned enterprises. Additionally, the dynamic development of business groups is also the result of foreign direct investments and the emergence of international entities expanding their activities in Poland (Romanowska, 1998). Increased dynamics of business groups' formation was observed in the 2000s, after Poland's accession to the European Union. Those business groups have their roots in private enterprises looking for opportunities to allocate excess financial resources in new markets and industries. According to Statistics Poland, over 2/3 of all business groups operating at the end of 2020 were established in the years 2004–2018 (Enterprise groups in Poland in 2020, 2022).

Types of Business Groups

There are many classifications of a business group in the literature. Among the numerous criteria, there are those relating to the ownership, internal organisation, role of the parent company, scope of operations in terms of industries and geographical markets, or size of the group. In this part, three generic classifications from the literature and one specific for Poland are discussed. The first one is the most common and is based on the ownership of a business group. The second classification distinguishes business groups according to the internal organisation referring to horizontal as well as vertical linkages between subsidiaries. The third is based mostly on behavioural principles adopted by constituent companies of business groups. The fourth is specific to the Polish literature and categorises business groups in respect to the role of the parent company.

The first classification is based on ownership of a business group. According to Cuervo-Cazurra (2006), three types of business groups can be distinguished: widely held, state-owned, and family-owned. In family-owned business groups, the individual or family are involved in ownership, control, and management of a business group. This type includes Korean *chaebols*, Latin American *groups economicos*, and Indian *business houses*. In family-owned business groups, family goals converge and intertwine with goals of a business group. The main goals of such business groups are the group's value growth, maintenance of independence, but also to ensure a source of income (and jobs) for the family in the future. A typical feature of those entities is the lack of separation of ownership from control and management. This results in a different specificity of internal processes of family-owned groups. For example, the decision-making process is less formalised and often takes place outside the office (Cuervo-Cazurra, 2006; Aluchna, 2010).

In state-owned business groups, the ownership is legally granted to citizens of the country, as they are owned by the government at a national (or sub-national) level. Their main purpose is to provide certain goods and services meeting needs of citizens. Such groups often operate in industries that are strategic for the country. Unfortunately, a disadvantage is that they are highly susceptible to a lack of professional management due to a political nomination of key positions. Another weakness of state-owned business groups is the multitude of goals (including non-business) and their dynamic change along with changes in the government. On the other hand, business groups of this type are less exposed to bankruptcy, often have access to preferential loans, and have priority in public procurement (Cuervo-Cazurra, 2006; Aluchna, 2010).

The last type is a widely held business group with a fragmented shareholder structure and absence of a majority shareholder. Ownership is distributed among many shareholders. Management is delegated to professional managers and there is a separation between ownership, control, and management. Those groups show greater pro-investment orientation and have an effective management and motivation systems. However, conflicts between shareholders and managers can arise. Those groups are common in many economies. Examples include the Japanese *keiretsu* and bank-centred business groups (Cuervo-Cazurra, 2006; Aluchna, 2010).

The next classification of a business group focuses on horizontal and vertical linkages within a business group. The horizontal link between affiliates relates to their role within the business group. Low degree of interdependence of strategic actions taken by affiliated firms is observed in business groups with loose horizontal linkages. In such business groups, affiliates often operate in different industries and locations with little in common in terms of resources and capabilities. In business groups with tighter horizontal connection between affiliated firms, high degree of interdependence of affiliates is observed and the strategic management in one firm influences other. The second type of a linkage within a business group, vertical one, relates to the relationship between the parent company and affiliates. When vertical linkage is tight, the parent company holds shares and controls rights of all affiliates, while the loose vertical linkage means that entities are connected more by social ties or control of resources (Yiu et al., 2007).

Yiu et al. (2007) distinguish four types of a business group according to the tightness of horizontal and vertical linkages: network (N-form), club (C-form), holding (H-form), and multidivisional (M-form). N-form business groups are characterised by tight horizontal and loose vertical linkages. The leader of a business group often operates in one industry, while other affiliated firms support it as suppliers of technology, intermediate products or services, and other functions. In this type of a business group social relations are key. The leader controls partners through interfirm transactions rather than ownership ties. An example of this type of a business group is the *guanxi qiye* in Taiwan.

C-form of a business group is related to lose horizontal as well as vertical linkages. This type of a business group is often very complex as it is represented by large corporations with a great number of subsidiaries. Affiliated firms are linked through a formal president club or a brand name rather than strong ownership ties. This business group is a kind of a platform for resource sharing. An example of a C-form business group is the Japanese *keiretsu*.

H-form business groups are related to tight vertical and lose horizontal connectedness. Those business groups are often highly diversified. The parent company acts as the headquarter and invests in affiliates that operate in different industries. Regarding the core subsidiaries, which provide major revenue for the group, the parent company implements more direct control over management via vertical ownership structure or corporate pyramid. Typical examples of H-form business groups are large conglomerates in Hong-Kong and business groups in France.

The last type of a business group, M-form, is characterised by tight horizontal and vertical linkages. The parent company acts as the headquarter by investing in affiliated firms that are organised according to its strategic objectives. Both vertical linkage and social relations are important because subsidiaries operate in related industries and there is a need for resources and competencies sharing. Internal transactions are very intensive in those business groups. Examples of M-form business groups are Korean *chaebols*, Belgian industrial business groups, and family-controlled groups in Italy.

The third classification, delivered by Colpan and Hikino (2010), is based predominantly on behavioural principles adopted by constituent companies of a business group. They distinguish two types of a business group with "alliance" and "authority" principles. The first is a network-type business group. It is a kind of lose coalition of legally independent companies that have common long-term goals. There is no single controlling owner and control unit. Thus, no one has dominant control over strategic and financial decisions of the whole business group, but rather there is administrative control based on the inter-firm coordination. This type is often called a business network. Thus, it is not an unequivocal example of a business group. However, some researchers indicate it as a business group.

Hierarchy-type business groups, based on an authority principle, are perceived as typical business groups. The authority principle makes a business group a coherent organisation model, in which the holding company controls affiliated firms. In a hierarchy-type business group, a family or entrepreneur own the parent company, although sometimes family-entrepreneurs control directly affiliated units. Coplan and Hikino (2010) mention two types of a hierarchy-type business group: diversified and pyramidal business groups. Diversified business group consists of legally independent companies that operate in numerous industries, often unrelated. Those companies are bound together by persistent (equity) and informal (family) ties. Diversified business groups often emerge as a response to market imperfections and are described from the perspective of development economics and strategy research. Pyramidal business group is the focus of the finance and governance literature. It consists of listed companies forming a pyramid in which one listed firm is a controlled subsidiary of another. Listed companies are under common control of the largest shareholder with at least 20% of votes. Common control can be pursued differently i.e. through direct or horizontal ownership, dual-class shares, and super voting stocks. A disproportion of equity ownership can therefore be observed, and an eventual exercise of dominant control of tiers of listed companies. This separation of control rights from cash-flow rights creates potential harm for minority shareholders.

Classification that is based on the parent company's role within a business group is very popular in the Polish literature. It distinguishes three types of a business group: operational, strategic, and financial ones (Trocki, 2004). The role of the parent company within the operational business group is crucial, because it carries out key operating activities in the group. This type of a business group has concentric interdependence as all activities of its subsidiaries are aimed at supporting the parent company in achieving the best possible market and financial performance. This type of a business group requires a significant level of integration and intensive coordination of activities due to intense linkages between subsidiaries and the parent company.

The dominant role of the parent company within a strategic business group is to exploit synergy and strategically manage subsidiaries that are operationally interlinked. Synergy is expected because of the integration of subsidiaries' activities. Operational links within a strategic business group emerge intensively between subsidiaries and are based on the sequential or mutual interdependence. The parent company focuses on managing, controlling, and coordinating activities of subsidiaries via financial and strategic decisions.

The last type of a business group in this classification is a financial business group. The parent company in financial business groups does not conduct operational activities as it is focused on managing shares held. The dominant type of group management is portfolio management. The main goal of the parent company is to maximise the return on investment in subsidiaries but simultaneously to diversify the investment risk. The parent company follows the same principles as other market investors, looking for optimal investment solutions from the perspective of risk and rate of return on invested capital.

Business Groups in Poland

The analysis of business groups in Poland is carried out based on data collected by Statistics Poland as it has been carrying out the systematic research on business groups in Poland since 2008. A business group is defined as a set of enterprises that are legally independent but rely on each other economically due to the control and/or ownership links between them. This definition is in line with broader business group definitions. Thus, statistics collected and delivered by Statistics Poland enable a deeper understanding of business groups operating in Poland.

Figure 1.1 presents changes in the number of business groups in Poland and those classified as national (business groups with subsidiaries that are residents in Poland) and international (both domestically controlled truncated group with subsidiaries located abroad and foreign controlled truncated group as a part of international group). Statistics clearly show that the number of business groups in the Polish economy increased significantly from 1,462 to 2,345 between 2008 and 2020 (increase by over 60.4% with CAGR of 4.5%). This dynamic increase in the number of business groups was accompanied by changes in their ways of functioning, ownership, employment, profitability, and so on.

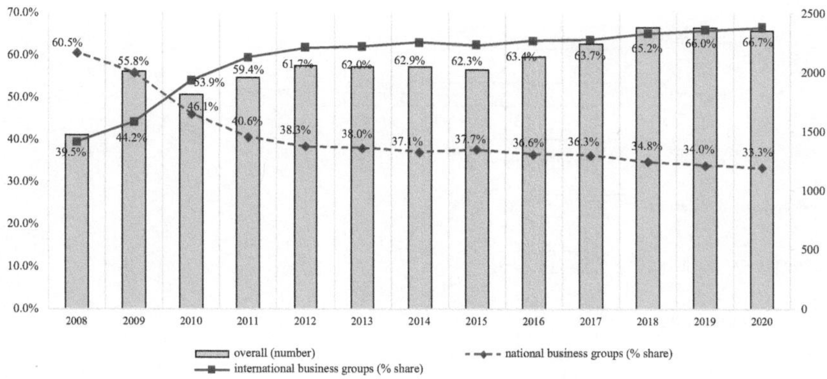

Figure 1.1 Business groups in Poland in 2008–2020.
Source: Own elaboration based on data from Statistics Poland.

Figure 1.1 also presents a systematic decline in the share of national business groups in total number of business groups in Poland. The number of national business groups decreased by 103 groups between 2008 and 2020, but with the dynamic increase in the number of international business groups, this translated into a decrease in the share in all business groups from 60.5% to 33.3%. In the analysed period, the number of international business groups increased by 986 groups showing an increase in their total share from 39.5% to 66.7%. This is the result of two trends. The first is the entrance of foreign business groups to Poland either organically or by acquiring business groups owned by domestic shareholders, and the second is the internationalisation of Polish business groups. The internationalisation strategy is commonly used, and more and more national business groups implement it. Some of them are important regional players like Maspex in the food industry or PKN Orlen in the oil industry. Others are also successful outside the CEE region, like Selena in construction chemicals, LPP in the fashion industry or Mercator Medical in the disposable medical supplies industry.

Figure 1.2 presents data on the ownership structure of business groups in Poland in 2020. It shows that the ownership structure in Poland is different than in Western Europe or Asia due to diversified paths of the formation of business groups in Poland. Among the business groups in Poland those with State Treasury ownership still prevail. Stated-owned business groups operate in strategic industries for the country, such as oil, gas, energy, and mining. Business groups of this type are usually large entities with very high employment. The second significant group of owners are foreign persons as Poland is an attractive market due to its geographical location and size of the domestic market, which attract foreign investments. In the ownership structure of business groups in Poland, other types of

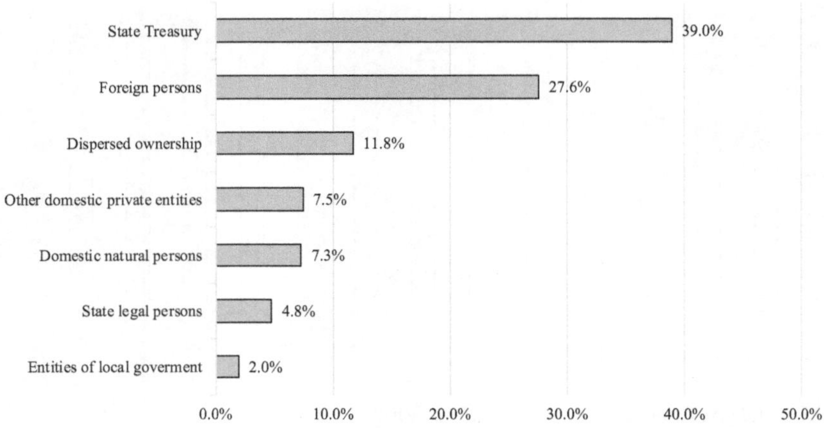

Figure 1.2 The ownership structure of business groups in Poland in 2020.
Source: Own elaboration based on data from Statistics Poland.

ownerships are less significant. However, the developing capital market positively influence the growing importance of dispersed ownership.

Figure 1.3 presents the share of business groups from three main industries in total number of business groups in Poland between 2008 and 2020 as they dominate certain industries. In Poland, business groups can be found most often in manufacturing, trade and repair of motor vehicles, and construction industries as they accounted for 56.7% of all business groups in 2020. The presence of business groups is natural in traditional and capital-intensive industries; however, their importance in those industries has been decreasing. They constituted as much as 65.6% of all business groups in 2008, and since 2012 their share has dropped below 60%. It shows that business groups have been becoming common also in other industries. Interestingly, almost 10% of business groups operated in professional, scientific, and technical activities in 2020, and it may represent a shift towards a knowledge-based economy.

Business groups differ also in terms of employment. They, most often, are perceived as large entities that employed hundreds or even thousands of people, but small business groups also exist. Figure 1.4 presents the share of business groups according to different employment classes in the total number of business groups in Poland between 2009 and 2020.[1] Figure 1.4 shows that business groups in Poland are mainly small- and medium-sized ones. Among all business groups, the largest share is held by those employing up to 49 people, and those with employment between 50 and 249. Those business groups accounted for over 59.4% in the total number of business groups in 2020. The domination of small- and medium-sized business groups is in line with the global trend. In other European

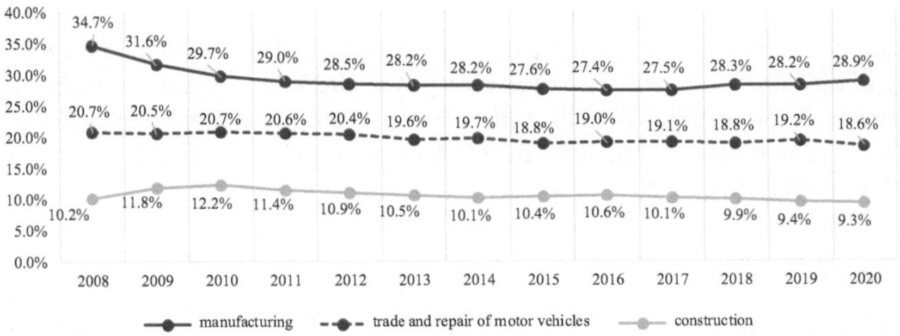

Figure 1.3 The share of business groups from the three most important industries in total number of business groups 2008–2020.

Source: Own elaboration based on data from Statistics Poland.

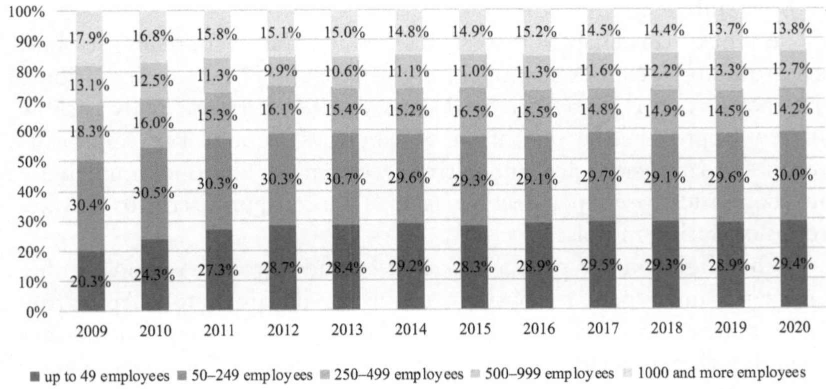

Figure 1.4 The share of business groups according to different employment classes in the total number of business groups in Poland in 2009–2020.

Source: Own elaboration based on data from Statistics Poland.

countries, smaller business groups are also more common, and their share in the total number of business group has been growing (Mierzejewska et al., 2015). It may be due to the popularity of a business group as a form of running a business, benefits of operating as a business group, but also possibility to operate on a large scale with low employment in the age of digitisation, automation, and virtualisation.

Business groups have a very strong impact on the economy. Statistics Poland's data show their significant role in the Polish economy. Entities belonging to business groups employed over 52.5% of employees of all non-financial enterprises in 2020. Their share of revenue in total revenue of all non-financial enterprises was 67.0%, and the gross financial result was 54.0% in 2020. That said, entities belonging to those business groups accounted for only 15.3% of all non-financial enterprises in 2020.

In addition, over 79.8% of 890 business groups that consolidated financial statements in 2020 achieved gross profit and 78.5% of them net profit in 2020. The profitability ratios also prove the effectiveness of business groups as those that consolidated financial statements obtained 4.3% of ROE (return on equity), 1.7% of ROA (return on assets), and 2.5% of net sales profitability in 2020.

Conclusion

The activity of business groups in different geographical regions has been one of the most interesting and constantly developing research issues. This is mainly due to the variety of their types and reasons for the creation of those entities but also their growing importance in the global economy. Business groups are analysed from an economic (including management), legal, political, or sociological perspectives. Unfortunately, they have still not been sufficiently recognised.

The aim of this chapter is to shed lights on the phenomenon of business groups, especially those operating in Poland. Thus, the definition of a business group is firstly briefly discussed. The literature analysis shows different approaches to definition of a business group. Two approaches prevail – broad sociological and narrow economics. This book implements the economics-based perspective as it is more appropriate to business groups operating in Poland.

To shed light on the phenomenon of business groups, reasons of their emergence and types of a business group are discussed too. Apart from the four most common approaches explaining the existence of business groups (market imperfection, cultural heritage, political economy, agency theory), the most common path of Polish business groups emergence is also presented. The dynamic transformation and growth of Polish economy resulted in business groups with different roots and history. Some of business groups are old state-owned entities; other were established at the beginning of the economic transformation in 1990s of the XX century (often because of privatisation), and still there are quite young entities owned by private and foreign investors as well as families.

This chapter presents different typologies of a business group showing the diversity of this organisational model. The most popular typology is based on the ownership criteria, which allows to identify widely held, state-owned, and family-owned business groups. Other studies deliver typologies of a business group based on internal organisation, size or behavioural principles, and others. A frequently used typology of Polish business groups distinguishes operational, strategic, and financial business groups that differ in terms of the role of the parent company within a business group.

The last part of the chapter characterises Polish business groups. It is a dynamic analysis that enables to identify significant changes over time.

Provided data give an insight into business group specificity. Despite the relatively small share of entities belonging to business groups in total number of non-financial enterprises, they are of a great importance in the Polish economy as employers providing many jobs and due to financial results. Business groups are profitable, operate in strategic industries, have many international links, and successfully operate on foreign markets.

To conclude, the analysis of business groups gives opportunities for researchers to enhance understanding of their internal mechanisms, organisation, and strategies. This research area has strong practical implications as business groups exist in different geographical regions and they have great impact on many local and regional economies.

Note

1 The analysis period was shortened due to the lack of data for 2008.

References

Almeida, H., Kim, C.S. & Kim, H.B. (2015). Internal capital markets in business groups: Evidence from the Asian financial crisis. *The Journal of Finance*, 70(6), 2539–2586.

Almeida, H., Park, S.Y., Subrahmanyam, M.G. & Wolfenzon, D. (2011). The structure and formation of business groups: Evidence from Korean chaebols. *Journal of Financial Economics*, 99(2), 447–475.

Aluchna, M. (2010). *Kierunki rozwoju polskich grup kapitałowych: Perspektywa międzynarodowa [Directions of growth of Polish business groups: International perspective].* Warszawa: Oficyna Wydawnicza SGH.

Barbero, M.I. & Puig, N. (2016). Business groups around the world: An introduction. *Business History*, 58(1), 6–29.

Carney, M., Gedajlovic, E.R., Heugens, P.P., Van Essen, M. & Van Oosterhout, J. (2011). Business group affiliation, performance, context, and strategy: A meta-analysis. *Academy of Management Journal*, 54(3), 437–460.

Chang, S.J. & Hong, J. (2002). How much does the business group matter in Korea? *Strategic Management Journal*, 23(3), 265–274.

Chung, C.N. (2001). Markets, culture and institutions: The emergence of large business groups in Taiwan, 1950s–1970s. *Journal of Management Studies*, 38(5), 719–745.

Claessens, S., Djankov, S., Fan, J.P. & Lang, H. P. (2002). Disentangling the incentive and entrenchment effects of large shareholdings. *The Journal of Finance*, 57(6), 2741–2771.

Collin, S.O. (1998). Why are these islands of conscious power found in the ocean of ownership? Institutional and governance hypotheses explaining the existence of business groups in Sweden. *Journal of Management Studies*, 35(6), 719–746.

Colpan, A.M. & Hikino, T. (2010). *Foundations of business groups: Towards and integrated framework*, in Colpan, A.M., Hikino, T. & Lincoln, J.R. (eds.) *The Oxford handbook of business groups.* Oxford: Oxford University Press.

Colpan, A.M. & Hikino, T. (eds.) (2018). *Business groups in the west. Origins, revolutions, and resilience.* Oxford: Oxford University Press.

Cuervo-Cazurra, A. (2006). Business groups and their types. *Asia Pacific Journal of Management*, 23(4), 419–437.

Cuervo-Cazurra, A. (2018). The evolution of business groups' corporate social responsibility. *Journal of Business Ethics*, 153(4), 997–1016.

Ćwik, K. (2013). Aspekty organizacji sieciowej a funkcjonowanie grupy kapitałowej [Aspects of the network organisation and the functioning of a business group]. *Kwartalnik Naukowy "Organizacja i Zarządzanie"*, 4(24), 29–41.

Dmowska, J. & Mikucka-Kowalczyk, M.A. (2019). Podstawowe założenia teorii organizacji sieciowych a aspekty funkcjonowania Grupy Kapitałowej KGHM [Basic assumptions of the theory of network organisations and aspects of the functioning of the KGHM Group]. *Ekonomìka ta mitno-pravovì vìdnosini*, 9–10, 12–22.

Encarnation, D. (1989). *Dislodging multinationals: India's comparative perspective.* Ithaca, NY: Cornell University Press.

Enterprise groups in Poland in 2020 (2022). Report of Statistics Poland, Poland.

Fisman, R. & Khanna, T. (2004). Facilitating development: The role of business groups. *World Development*, 32(4), 609–628.

Gonenc, H. & Hermes, N. (2008). Propping: Evidence from new share issues of Turkish business group firms. *Journal of Multinational Financial Management*, 18(-3), 261–275.

Granovetter, M. (1984). Small is bountiful: Labor markets and establishment size. *American Sociological Review*, 49(3), 323–334.

Granovetter, M. (1995). Coase revisited: Business groups in the modern economy. *Industrial and Corporate Change*, 4(1), 93–130.

Guillen, M.F. (2000). Business groups in emerging economies: A resource-based view. *Academy of Management Journal*, 43(3), 362–380.

Hsieh, T.J., Yeh, R.S. & Chen, Y.J. (2010). Business group characteristics and affiliated firm innovation: The case of Taiwan. *Industrial Marketing Management*, 39(4), 560–570.

Iacobucci, D. & Rosa, P. (2005). Growth, diversification, and business group formation in entrepreneurial firms. *Small Business Economics*, 25(1), 65–82.

Khanna, T. & Palepu, K. (1997). Why focused strategies. *Harvard Business Review*, 75(4), 41–51.

Khanna, T. & Palepu, K. (2000). Is group affiliation profitable in emerging markets? An analysis of diversified Indian business groups. *The Journal of Finance*, 55(2), 867–891.

Khanna, T. & Rivkin, J.W. (2001). Estimating the performance effects of business groups in emerging markets. *Strategic Management Journal*, 22(1), 45–74.

Khanna, T. & Rivkin, J.W. (2006). Interorganizational ties and business group boundaries: Evidence from an emerging economy. *Organization Science*, 17(3), 333–352.

Leff, N.H. (1978). Industrial organization and entrepreneurship in the developing countries: The economic groups. *Economic Development and Cultural Change*, 26(4), 661–675.

Luo, X. & Chung, C.N. (2005). Keeping it all in the family: The role of particularistic relationships in business group performance during institutional transition. *Administrative Science Quarterly*, 50(3), 404–439.

Maman, D. (2002). The emergence of business groups: Israel and South Korea compared. *Organization Studies*, 23(5), 737–758.

Mierzejewska, W., Dworzecki, Z. & Tomaszewski, A. (2015). Polskie grupy kapitałowe na tle europejskich [Polish business groups compared to other European ones], in Mierzejewska, W. & Dworzecki, Z. (eds.) *Zachowania polskich grup kapitałowych w czasach kryzysu [Behaviors of Polish business groups in times of crisis]*. Warszawa: Oficyna Wydawnicza SGH.

Popli, M., Ladkani, R.M. & Gaur, A.S. (2017). Business group affiliation and post-acquisition performance: An extended resource-based view. *Journal of Business Research*, 81, 21–30.

Romanowska, M. (1998). Strategie grup kapitałowych w Polsce [Strategies of business groups in Poland], in Romanowska, M., Trocki, M. & Wawrzyniak, B. (eds) *Grupy kapitałowe w Polsce [Business groups in Polnad]*. Warszawa: Difin.

Schneider, B.R. (2009). A comparative political economy of diversified business groups, or how states organize big business. *Review of International Political Economy*, 16(2), 178–201.

Singh, D.A. & Gaur, A.S. (2009). Business group affiliation, firm governance, and firm performance: Evidence from China and India. *Corporate Governance: An International Review*, 17(4), 411–425.

Sutherland, D. & Lutao, N. (2015). The emergence and evolution of Chinese business groups: Are pyramidal groups forming, in Barry, N. & Kellee, S.T. (eds.) *State capitalism, institutional adaptation, and the Chinese miracle*. New York: Cambridge University Press.

Trocki, M. (2004), *Grupy kapitałowe. Tworzenie i funkcjonowanie [Business groups. Emergence and functioning]*. Warszawa: PWN.

Yiu, D., Bruton, G.D. & Lu, Y. (2005). Understanding business group performance in an emerging economy: Acquiring resources and capabilities in order to prosper. *Journal of Management Studies*, 42(1), 183–206.Yiu, D.W., Lu, Y., Bruton, G.D. & Hoskisson, R.E. (2007). Business groups: An integrated model to focus future research. *Journal of Management Studies*, 44(8), 1551–1579.

Zhang, L., Sjögren, H. & Kishida, M. (2016). The emergence and organizational persistence of business groups in China, Japan, and Sweden. *Industrial and Corporate Change*, 26(6), 885–902.

2 Cooperation, Competition, and Coopetition within Business Groups

Wioletta Mierzejewska

Introduction

The modern economy has led to the intensification and simultaneous transformation of relationships between companies. Relationships with suppliers, customers, and competitors have become reoriented due to high variability and unpredictability of a business environment. Strengthening industry links with companies, both internally and externally, is perceived as a key element of the strategy dealing with an uncertain environment. According to Moore and Curry (1996), the traditional struggle with competitors is a thing of the past, and firms should evolve along with the business environment and enter new forms of relationships with competitors. Bengtsson and Kock (1999) indicate four types of relationships between firms: coexistence, competition, cooperation, and coopetition. Apart from coexistence, those types of relations concern intensive economical, informational, and social interactions. Competition and cooperation are well-known relationships that have been examined from various perspectives, e.g. economic, sociological, psychological, or political. It seems that the most interesting and, at the same time, most complicated type of a relation between firms is coopetition, which is understood as something between "pure cooperation and pure competition" (Osarenkhoe, 2010: 343), and means the coexistence and interdependence of competition and cooperation. Although cooperation and competition were previously considered to be mutually exclusive relationships, impossible to exist at the same time, business practice has shown that even the biggest rivals (e.g. Coca-Cola and Pepsi, Apple and Samsung) cooperate in certain activities.

Coopetition refers to a complex structure of interdependencies between firms, in which cooperation and competition are simultaneously present and related to each other (Dagnino & Padula, 2002). It is a way to define a strategic game in an industry based on the simultaneous economic and non-economic exchange (Brandenburger & Nalebuff, 1996). It cannot, therefore, be considered by neither the development of competition theory nor cooperation theory, but a completely new type of inter- and intra-organisational relations (Yami et al., 2010). The theoretical frameworks

DOI: 10.4324/9781003324775-3

used to study coopetition are game theory, transaction cost theory, and resource-based view (Dal-Soto & Monticelli, 2017).

Coopetition is a frequently used theory explaining complex relations between and within organisations. It is commonly found within business groups that consist of formally independent firms (subsidiaries, affiliates) under the same administrative and financial control (Leff, 1978; Chan & Hong, 2002). Affiliated companies are linked by various ties, including ownership, personal, and commercial ones (Chung, 2001; Yiu et al., 2005) that cause the emergence of a strategic interdependence (Luo, 2005). Additionally, affiliates pursue goals of the whole business group as well as individual ones. It induces individual units to compete to meet different goals and strategic priorities and at the same time cooperate in the interest of the whole organisation.

Previous studies proved that in complex organisations, such as multinational corporations or business groups, collaborative and competitive ties between units exist (Tsai, 2002; Luo, 2005; Tippmann et al., 2018; Liu et al., 2019). However, internal relationships within business groups have still not been thoroughly examined. By building on the coopetition theory, this chapter, therefore, gives insights into relationships between subsidiaries within a business group and answers the question whether coopetition is a frequent relationship in business groups and what are its features. Research results covered by this chapter contribute both to the coopetition and business group research streams.

Theoretical Lenses

Essence of Coopetition

Coopetition, as a new type of a relationship between entities, has gained considerable attention in the management literature (Bouncken et al., 2020; Czakon et al., 2020; Gernsheimer et al., 2021) since it was introduced by Brandenburger and Nalebuff (1996). In their early work, Bengtsson and Kock describe it as "a relationship simultaneously containing elements of both cooperation and competition" (1999: 178). Thus, coopetition combines two types of relationships that usually involve strongly opposing logic (Dorn et al., 2016) and is based on partial interest and goal congruence. This creates a paradoxical situation in which firms compete in some activities and cooperate in others (Chiambaretto et al., 2020). Firms are very often more willing to cooperate in upstream activities of the value chain that are located further from the client, i.e. production, logistics, technology development, and R&D activities while competition can more often be found in downstream activities of the value chain that are located closer to the client, i.e. sales, product positioning, or marketing (Bengtsson & Kock, 2000; Kotzab & Teller, 2003). In modern approaches, coopetition is perceived as an interplay between competition and cooperation manifested through mutual pursuits, resource leverage, safeguarded resources, and relevant commitments (Gnyawali & Charleton, 2018) and is presented as the best strategic option that can create a win-win situation for all parties involved (Le Roy & Czakon, 2016). Coopetition is also considered as organisational paradox (Ricciardi et al., 2021), orthogonal constructs (Bengtsson et al., 2010), dynamic process, and important strategy in an unpredictable environment (Köseoğlu et al., 2018).

Coopetition can be defined through its features. Two of them – simultaneity and value creation – are perceived as core elements of the coopetition theory (Gnyawali & Charleton, 2018; Gernsheimer et al., 2021). Simultaneity means that cooperation and competition are found between the same players at the same time. Thus, coopetition must be distinguished from a situation where there is a sequence of competition and cooperation between firms. Simultaneity is closely related to intensity and magnitude of cooperation and competition, and some researchers argue that only balanced coopetition (with evenness between cooperation and competition) leads to a positive influence on value creation (Gnyawali & Charleton, 2018). In most approaches to coopetition, it is indicated that entities engage in a coopetition relationship with value creation intend. Value creation means superior performance and additional benefits compared to other relational modes (Gnyawali & Charleton, 2018; Chiambaretto et al., 2020) because of mutual efforts and pursuits form all coopeting partners (Santos, 2021). The aim of coopetition is to bring benefits for all players involved (Czakon et al., 2014). Value creation appears when firms exchange knowledge to create more value than they could do alone (Gernsheimer et al., 2021). Additionally, apart from creating value, interesting issue is its appropriation, which means understanding how common value is captured and shared among individual partners (Gernsheimer et al., 2021). Other features of coopetition often found in the literature are complexity, variability, dynamic, managerial challenges, and industry reshaping (Czakon et al., 2014).

Competition and cooperation relationships are often placed at the ends of one continuum or as two separate continuums (Bengtsson et al., 2010). This enables to make a distinction of different types of coopetition according to intensity of cooperation and competition. Bengtsson and Kock (2000) propose three types of coopetition relationship: competition-dominated (when competition prevails over cooperation), cooperation-dominated (when cooperation prevails over competition), and balanced coopetition (when cooperation and competition are equally distributed). Other typology, proposed by Luo (2004), delivers four types of coopetition relationship based on the cooperation and competition intensity placed on two separated continuums. Those are contender (high competition and low cooperation), estranger (low competition and low cooperation), partner (low competition and high cooperation), and integrator (high competition and high cooperation). This typology has been developed with reference to the relationship between multinational corporations and local governance. Each type of coopetition consists of various strategic tactics that relate to both the firm's goals and the bargaining power resulting from the resources held.

Coopetition has found substantial resonance on all levels of analysis, such as individual (Hutter et al., 2011; Baruch & Lin, 2012), inter-organisational (Gnyawali & Park, 2009; Kylänen & Rusko, 2011), intra-organisational (Luo, 2005; Luo et al., 2006), and network (Gnyawali et al., 2006; Peng & Bourne, 2009). Individual coopetition occurs between employees (Dorn et al., 2016), while intra-organisational coopetition refers to simultaneous cooperation and competition between subunits, groups, or teams within one organisation (Dorn et al., 2016; Bendig et al., 2018; An & Kreutzer, 2020; Chen et al., 2020). Intra-organisational coopetition may occur within one single organisation (between departments) or a business group/multiunit organisation, where subsidiaries/subunits need to cooperate with each other and at the same time compete deliberately. Inter-organisational coopetition is portrayed by simultaneous cooperation and competition between two (dyadic coopetition) or more independent firms (network coopetition) (Dagnino, 2009; Czakon & Czernek, 2016) and is the best recognised area in the coopetition studies (Dorn et al., 2016; Gernsheimer et al., 2021). Network coopetition occurs within networks (Gnyawali et al., 2006) and between different networks (Peng & Bourne, 2009).

Coopetition relationship generates different positive outcomes and tensions as well. Benefits of coopetition include obtaining resources, knowledge creation and acquisition, risk and cost sharing, product and services development, competitive advantage improvement, economics of scale and scope, market power, easier internationalisation, and others (Ritala et al., 2014; Bouncken et al., 2015; Bengtsson & Raza-Ullah, 2016; Devece et al., 2019; Gernsheimer et al., 2021). Coopetition also influences better innovation performance (Bouncken & Kraus, 2013; Park et al., 2014) and enhances market performance (Robert et al., 2018). However, research results on the relationship between coopetition and company's performance show mixed results (Chiambaretto et al., 2020). The explanation of those mixed results are tensions triggered by coopetition at different levels. Coopetition can be a win-win strategy, yet it could also be a win-lose strategy due to tensions related to cooperation with competitors (Le Roy & Czakon, 2016). Coopetition can lead to asymmetry of benefits, create opportunistic behaviour and conflicts, lead to knowledge leakage, loss of organisational independence, and others (Tidström, 2014; Cygler et al., 2018; Santos, 2021). To benefit from simultaneous cooperation and competition, this relation should, therefore, be managed carefully (Le Roy & Czakon, 2016).

Coopetition Patterns within Business Groups

Affiliated companies, like independent firms, interact in various ways. They may not only coexist with nearly no economic, information, and social exchange (that is rare) but also intensively cooperate and compete. Previous studies proved that subsidiaries within business groups enter into competitive and cooperative relationships of different intensity and scope with other subsidiaries (Hong & Snell, 2015; Amata et al., 2021). Due to the specificity of business groups, the fundamental relationship linking affiliated companies is cooperation (Song et al., 2016; Tippmann et al., 2018; Chen & Tsou, 2020). It can be defined as a joint action undertaken by the parent company and subsidiaries in different areas and directions, both horizontally and vertically (Mierzejewska & Dziurski, 2021).

The most often indicated areas of cooperation between subsidiaries are technological, operational, organisational, and financial (Luo, 2005). Cooperation within business groups covers cross-selling, common infrastructure, joint purchase and distribution, sharing resources and knowledge, common investments, and financing policies (Cygler et al., 2012). The opportunity to cooperate creates affiliates' diversity of resources and capabilities (Chang & Hong, 2000). The intensity of cooperation between subsidiaries differs according to the type and profile of a business group (Mierzejewska & Dziurski, 2021). For example, a low intensity of internal cooperation characterises business groups with differentiated subsidiaries' profiles due to low synergy potential (Dellestrand et al., 2020), while a high intensity of internal cooperation can be found within business groups with a dominant, operational role of the parent company and supportive role of subsidiaries that are mutually interdependent.

Cooperation within business groups is needed to gain global efficiency, exchange knowledge, or lead joint projects (Luo, 2005; Mudambi, 2011; Liu et al., 2019). Cooperation enables subsidiaries to deal with market imperfections, generate economies of scale and scope, create and develop knowledge, and generally achieve goals set by the parent company (Tippmann et al., 2018). It manifests through knowledge and resource sharing (Kasper & Mühlbacher, 2008; Haas & Cummings, 2015; Tippmann et al., 2017; Chiambaretto et al., 2019; Zhang et al., 2019) and is expressed in business group internal markets (Birkinshaw & Fey, 2000; Cerrato, 2006; Enright & Subramanian, 2007).

During the long life of such complex organisations as business groups, apart from cooperation, other relationships between subsidiaries appear, and one of them being competition. Competition within a business group covers different areas. It could be product-market competition as well as competition for scarce resources, such as technology, capital, and people or support and attention of the parent company and position within the group (Birkinshaw & Lingblad, 2005; Luo, 2005; Chambers, 2015; Tippmann et al., 2018; Liu et al., 2019; Dellestrand et al., 2020; Lagerström et al.,

2021). Internal competition emerges also due to the charter overlap and development of subsidiaries' resources and competencies (Birkinshaw & Lingblad, 2001; Lagerström et al., 2021). It is, sometimes, related to the competence gap between units and knowledge flow (Rugman & Verbke, 2001; Tsai, 2002). Competition may be initiated by subsidiaries that pursue their own goals and want to improve their position and outperform others in a business group (Amata et al., 2021), or it could be the result of the parent company actions. Those could be restructuring activities consisting of shifting resources and competences between subsidiaries with similar profiles. It could also be the effect of parent company assessment of subsidiaries' ability to achieve goals of the whole business group. This results in competition aimed at ensuring the growth of the subsidiaries' strategic value for the whole business group (Fong et al., 2007; Becker-Ritterspach & Dörrenbächer, 2009, 2011).

Cooperation and competition emerging between subsidiaries make up the coopetition within a business group. Competition is a relationship that constitutes coopetition in business groups as cooperation is a natural relationship that connects subsidiaries. Coopetition within business groups is understood as the simultaneous pursuit of internal cooperative and competitive actions by subsidiaries. Some researchers argue that coopetition is central to the operation of business groups, especially those with geographically dispersed units (Luo, 2005; Hong & Snell, 2015; Tippmann et al., 2018). The coopetitive relationships in a business group may appear horizontally (between subsidiaries) and vertically (between the parent company and subsidiaries) (Schmid & Maurer, 2011). Thus, the coopetition network may cover the entire business group, but it may also connect only selected subsidiaries. Subsidiaries with unique competences and resources can be a frequent cooperation partner for others, while those insufficiently equipped with resources, operating on similar markets, or having ambitious managers, may more often enter competitive relations with sister-subsidiaries.

Coopetition between subsidiaries can be recognised by the degree of subsidiaries' cooperation and competition (Tippmann et al., 2018). Therefore, cooperation-dominated, competition-dominated, as well as balanced coopetition can be found in business groups (Bengtsson & Kock, 2000; Gnyawali & Charleton, 2018; Bouncken et al., 2020). Luo (2005) delivers a conceptual model of internal coopetition within a multinational enterprise with different types of coopetition regarding intensity of cooperation and competition. In this model, some subsidiaries enter relationships with a high intensity of both cooperation and competition, while others may prefer relationships with a high intensity of cooperation, but low intensity of competition. Therefore, due to the intensity of competition and cooperation, the following categories of subsidiaries can be distinguished: aggressive demander (high intensity of competition and low intensity of cooperation), silent implementer (low intensity of competition and low intensity of cooperation), ardent contributor (low intensity of competition and high intensity of cooperation), and network captain (high intensity of competition and high intensity of cooperation). Each subsidiary within a business group may have a different coopetition identity with other subsidiaries. Additionally, subsidiaries roles are dynamic and change over time.

Coopetition within business groups is partly a created relationship, but it also appears spontaneously as an effect of the development of a business group. In some situations, the parent company induces and incentivises internal coopetition to gain better results (Luo, 2005, 2007; Song et al., 2016; Lagerström et al., 2021). For example, in hypercompetitive and hypertechnological environments, coopetition between affiliates enables an increase in innovativeness and gaining a competitive advantage (Song et al., 2016). Additionally, coopetition can emerge unintentionally during the long life of a business group, because managers of individual subsidiaries undertake strategic activities to achieve own goals (Cantwell and Mudambi, 2005; Ciabuschi et al., 2012; Mierzejewska, 2018).

Coopetition relationship in business groups is different from the inter-organisational coopetition due to ownership ties between subsidiaries, bargaining power of players engaged in the coopetition, determinants of business group emergence, and possibilities of managing this relationship. The specificity of this relationship within business groups is related to the specificity of the engaged players. Subsidiaries are not independent entities with full autonomy and decision-making freedom. The scopes of tasks, goals, and strategies are usually imposed top-down. At the level of the entire group, control and coordination mechanisms are also implemented, which is another factor limiting the freedom of subsidiaries. Under such conditions, coopetition within business groups is of a different character, intensity, and course than inter-organisational coopetition. This makes it an interesting phenomenon, worth further exploration.

Empirical Findings

The study, which results are presented in the chapter, uses a survey database of 121 business groups in Poland that was drawn from the databases of business groups that the parent company is listed on the Warsaw Stock Exchange. Data were acquired from surveys with top managers of parent companies from randomly selected business groups, Amadeus database and financial statements published by business groups. Information about the research sample and method is presented in the introduction. Research results on cooperation, competition, and coopetition in Polish business groups are discussed below.

The assessment of coopetition is made by decomposing this relation into cooperation and competition as it was done in previous studies (Tsai & Hsu, 2014; Bendig et al., 2018; Liu et al., 2019). The intensity of both dynamics was operationalised using a unidimensional measure and single-item scale (Ritala, 2012; Zakrzewska-Bielawska, 2013). The surveyed managers of parent companies were asked to separately assess the intensity of competition and cooperation between subsidiaries in a business group on a five-point Likert-type scale (1 – very low intensity, 5 – very high intensity). As assumed, the intensity of cooperation is very high. The mean is 4.215, median and mode are 4. Over 87.6% of respondents assessed it as high or very high. Interestingly, no respondent assessed the intensity of cooperation in business group as very low, and only one as low. In contrast to cooperation, most of the respondents (73.6%) assessed competition within a business group as very low and low. At the same time, no respondents assessed the intensity of competition between subsidiaries as high or very high. The mean is 1.843, median 2, and mode 1. It can, therefore, be concluded that competition between subsidiaries is present, but not on a large scale.

The superimposition of competition and cooperation assessments allows for the delivery of coopetition types based on the intensity of those relations. An aggregation of ratings was made. Rating of 1 (very low) and 2 (low) is identified as low intensity, rating of 3 as medium, and rating of 4 (high) and 5 (very high) as high intensity of both cooperation and competition. This allows for a presentation of nine potential types of coopetition regarding its intensity (Figure 2.1).

Two types of coopetition within business groups dominate in the surveyed sample. The first is coopetition with low intensity of competition

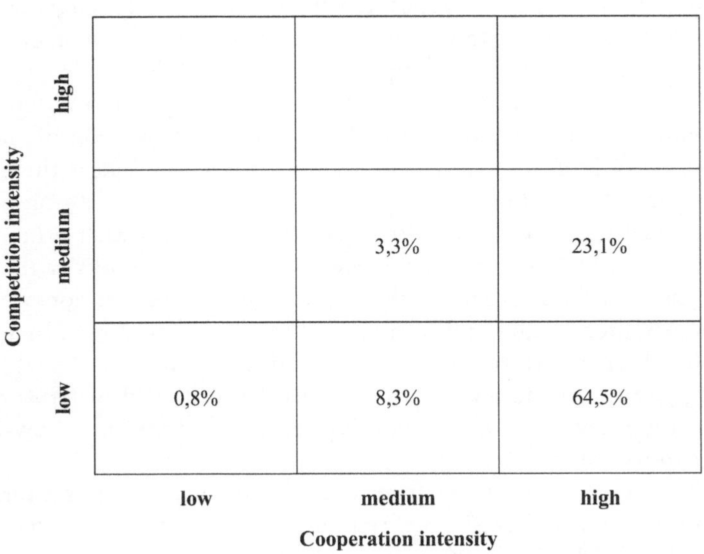

Figure 2.1 Nine-field coopetition matrix considering cooperation and competition intensities.

Source: Own elaboration.

and high intensity of cooperation. Over 64.5% of respondents indicated such a combination of cooperation and competition in their business groups. This means that the coopetition relation between subsidiaries within business groups, according to Bengtsson and Kock (2000), should be classified as cooperation-dominated coopetition or, according to Luo (2004), as partner coopetition. This type of coopetition is favoured by the complementarity of resources and skills of partners with market separation. Such situation may take place within some business groups, in which subsidiaries are created for different purposes and equipped with complementary resources, and their operations are strictly controlled and coordinated by the parent company. This is clearly visible in operational business groups, in which subsidiaries are connected by different types of interdependence. In the study, most of business groups surveyed are classified as operational or strategic-operational ones, in which the parent company conducts intensive operating activities. Those types of business groups form a tight network of intensively cooperating entities. Coopetition with domination of cooperation is, therefore, expected as prevailing in business groups. Despite low level of competition between entities, cooperation is still the main relationship between subsidiaries forming a business group.

The second type, much less frequently indicated by respondents, although accounting for over one-fifth of responses, is coopetition of high intensity of cooperation and medium intensity of competition (23.1% of respondents). Since the indication of the medium intensity of competition is the highest indication on a 5-point scale, this type can be carefully considered as similar the balanced coopetition in the concept of Bengtsson and Kock (2000), or the integrator coopetition in the typology of Luo (2004). This is a very cautious assumption based on the belief that respondents were not inclined to mark higher levels of competition within business groups. It should be noted that the integrator coopetition often arises in the case of high mutual dependence of enterprises, where there is a need to cooperate to achieve above-average results. In case of business groups, individual subsidiaries are often very dependent on each other. At the same time, they all strive to achieve above-average results at the level of the entire business group. Both cooperation and competition are supposed to guarantee a higher performance of individual entities, which translates into a higher performance of entire business group.

Further aggregation of ratings allows to create a four-field matrix in which the medium level of both relationships is classified into the "low-intensity" category (Figure 2.2).

Figure 2.2 shows that the cooperation-dominated coopetition prevails in business groups surveyed as 87.6% of respondents indicated to this type. On the other hand, 12.4% of respondents indicated that in their business group interactions between subsidiaries are rare, both in terms of cooperation and competition. This may be related to the type of a business group. In case of business groups consisting of subsidiaries with differentiated

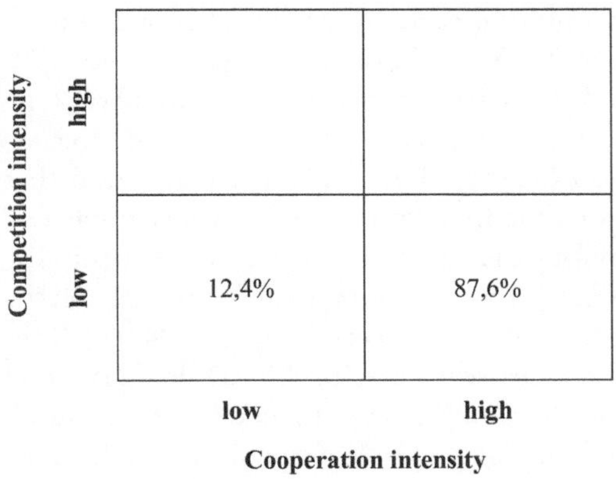

Figure 2.2 Four-field coopetition matrix considering cooperation and competition intensity.
Source: Own elaboration.

profiles, both cooperation and competition may be low (Dellestrand et al., 2020). A low potential to generate synergy effects does not encourage cooperation, while diversified products and good resources' equipment do not encourage competition.

Cooperation as well as competition within business groups can take place vertically and horizontally. Respondents were asked what type of cooperation and competition prevails in business groups: vertical (between subsidiaries and the parent company), horizontal (among subsidiaries themselves), or network (equally between subsidiaries and the parent company, and among subsidiaries themselves). According to data, most respondents indicated vertical cooperation (51.2%) and network competition (67.8%) as dominant. A joint analysis of answers to the question about the dominant direction of competition and cooperation allows for the identification of network and unidirectional coopetition. Unidirectional coopetition is identified if there is only vertical cooperation and competition at the same time, or only horizontal cooperation and competition at the same time. In contrast, network coopetition is identified in all other situations. In business groups surveyed, network coopetition is dominant. It is identified in 92.6% of business groups examined. This supports the view of intense and close relations between all entities forming a business group.

Another interesting issue is the area of cooperation and competition. Eleven areas of potential cooperation and competition have been identified in relation to Porter's (1985) value chain concept: production, logistics, sales, marketing, aftersales services, R&D, procurement, finance, IT, HR management, and storage. The first five activities are classified as primary activities, while the rest are classified as support activities. Managers surveyed were asked to assess whether there are cooperation and competition (vertical and horizontal) in each area. Vertical cooperation is predominantly found in finance (98.3% of business groups surveyed), IT (84.3%), marketing (81.8%), and aftersales services (81.8%), while horizontal is the most frequently indicated in sales (71.9%), procurement (68.6%), finance (62.8%), and production (62.0%). This leads to a conclusion that vertical cooperation focuses on support activities, while horizontal cooperation covers primary activities that may be carried out sequentially, and each subsidiary is responsible for a narrow part of operations. As for competition, the vertical one most often concerns finance (24.0%), HR management (12.4%), and after-sales services (10.7%), while horizontal competition focuses more on production (73.6%), finance (70.2%), and IT (40.5%). Superimposing areas of cooperation and competition enable identification in which area a coopetition relationship most often emerges. It turns out that vertical coopetition (simultaneous vertical cooperation and competition) can be found almost only in finance (24.0%). In other areas, it is incidental. The situation with horizontal coopetition (simultaneous horizontal cooperation and competition) is very different. It appears much more often in various areas although mainly in production (45.5%), procurement (27.3%), sales (25.6%), and finance (42.1%). Coopetition in the first three areas may be the result of overlapping subsidiaries or deliberate activities of the parent company to ensure an optimal level of product diversity by agreeing to partial product drainage. Coopetition in finance is explained in literature as cooperation that may relate to financing, transfer pricing, hedging against risk, internal financial initiatives (Luo, 2005), and "healthy competition" in terms of results (Schleimer & Riege, 2009).

An analysis of the number of cooperation and competition areas is the basis for identifying a simple and complex coopetition within business groups. The research on inter-organisational coopetition defines simple coopetition as cooperation with a competitor in only one area of the value chain (Czakon, 2014). The nature of a business group almost excludes the possibility of such situation; hence, a different approach is needed. Simple coopetition is equated with cooperation and competition in a small number of areas in the value chain. The limit (boundary) value in the research is the average number of cooperation and competition areas for the entire sample. If cooperation and competition are found below the average, it is classified as a narrow range of coopetition (simple coopetition), and all other combinations as broad coopetition (complex coopetition). As it was expected, the analysis proved that complex coopetition dominates in business groups surveyed. It is found in 63.6% of business groups surveyed, while simple coopetition, related to small number of cooperation and competition areas, is identified only in 36.4% of business groups surveyed.

The above consideration makes it possible to propose a classification of coopetition types according to the direction and number of areas in the value chain of coopetition (Figure 2.3). It is inspired by the classification

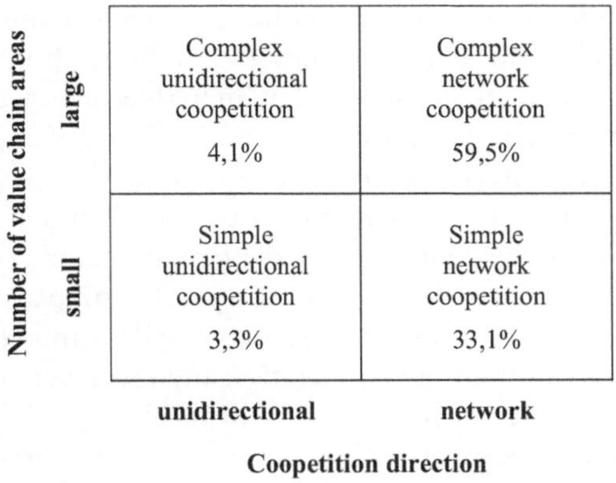

Figure 2.3 Coopetition matrix considering the coopetition direction and number of areas in the value chain.

Source: Own elaboration.

proposed by Dagnino and Padula (2002), who distinguish types of coopetitive relations based on the number of partners involved and number of areas in the value chain.

Figure 2.3 shows that among business groups surveyed, complex network coopetition dominates (59.5% of business groups surveyed). This means that simultaneous cooperation and competition can be noted in many directions, i.e. both vertically and horizontally, and in many areas of the value chain at the same time. The smallest number (3.3%) concerns an extremely different type, i.e. simple unidirectional coopetition. This conclusion supports the view about the network nature of business groups. The multiplicity of relations concerning various directions and areas, which can be found in business groups, also confirms the complexity of those entities.

Conclusion

The aim of this chapter is to expand the knowledge on relationships between subsidiaries within business groups from the perspective of coopetition theory. To show the phenomenon of coopetition within business groups research results on 121 business groups operating in Poland are presented. The main conclusion is that coopetition emerges within business groups surveyed. Findings from the study support previous research proving that both cooperative and competitive behaviours can be found within complex organisations, including business groups (Luo, 2005; Song et al., 2016; Tippmann et al., 2018; Liu et al., 2019). The dominant type of relationship within business groups surveyed shows a high intensity of cooperation and low intensity of competition. The main reason for such a result is the specificity of business groups that are created to achieve a common goal. This usually requires intensive cooperation within a whole organisation. Additionally, agency and resource dependency forces induce both cooperation and competition between subsidiaries, which role changes over time into excellence centres in business group networks (Zona et al., 2019; Chen & Tsuo, 2020). The internal embeddedness of subsidiaries also favours cooperation, and competition emerges only to a small extent. Competition in business groups can be controlled by the parent company; thus, it is not excessive. One of the main activities of the parent company are coordination and optimalisation of resource allocation (Dellestrand & Kappen, 2012) through which it can promote cooperation and low level of competition, therefore enhancing the effectiveness of subsidiaries.

Cooperation and competition take place within business groups horizontally as well as vertically. The research results show that cooperation is predominantly vertical, and competition is predominantly network (both vertical and horizontal). Superimposing cooperation and competition directions enables to prove that coopetition within business groups is mainly network. It supports the view of a business group as a network of interdependent firms that can engage to some extent independently in interfirm relations (Leff, 1978; Carney et al., 2011; Kim & Lui, 2015). According to this approach, subsidiaries benefit from multiple relations that emerge within business groups (Carney et al., 2011).

Business groups surveyed cooperate and compete in various areas of the value chain, both vertically and horizontally, and the study found out in which areas of the value chain there is simultaneous cooperation and competition. It turns out that both vertically and horizontally coopetition appears in finance. This supports the view of the importance of the internal capital market within a business group. Internal capital market imperatives are the relocation of finance across the group, risk sharing, and the influence of dividend policies of subsidiaries (He et al., 2013; Gopalan et al., 2014). Thus, cooperation and competition in finance are the most often observed within business groups. Horizontal coopetition is also found in production, procurement, and sales, which may be because there is process organisation of subsidiaries in surveyed business groups.

The joint analysis of the direction of coopetition and areas of the value chain, in which competition and cooperation within business groups take place, enables further insight into relationships between subsidiaries. The analysis is inspired by a classification proposed by Dagnino and Padula (2002). The research results show that the complex network coopetition is dominant within business groups. This type of coopetition is associated with multidirectional coopetition across many areas in the value chain. This means there are rather complicated relations of cooperation and competition within business groups. Numerous internal interactions are part of the network approach to business groups (Carney et al., 2011) and refer to the concept of subsidiaries' embeddedness in internal relations (Andersson & Forsgren, 1996).

References

Amata, R., Dagnino, G.B., Minà, A. & Picone, P.M. (2021). Managing coopetition in diversified firms: Insights from a qualitative case study. *Long Range Planning*, 55(4), 102128.

An, D. & Kreutzer, M. (2020). Employees' yin and yang mindset and intra-firm coopetition in growth companies. *Academy of Management Proceedings*, 2020(1), 19728.

Andersson, U. & Forsgren, M. (1996). Subsidiary embeddedness and control in a multinational corporation. *International Business Review*, 5(5), 487–508.

Baruch, Y. & Lin, C.P. (2012). All for one, one for all: Coopetition and virtual team performance. *Technological Forecasting and Social Change*, 79(6), 1155–1168.

Becker-Ritterspach, F., & Dörrenbächer, C. (2009). Intra-firm competition in multinational corporations: Towards a political framework. *Competition & Change*, 13(3), 199–213.

Becker-Ritterspach, F. & Dörrenbächer, C. (2011). An organizational politics perspective on intra-firm competition in multinational corporations. *Management International Review*, 51(4), 533–559.

Bendig, D., Enke, S., Thieme, N. & Brettel, M. (2018). Performance implications of cross-functional coopetition in new product development: The mediating role of organizational learning. *Industrial Marketing Management*, 73, 137–153.

Bengtsson, M. & Kock, S. (1999). Cooperation and competition in relationships between competitors in business networks. *Journal of Business & Industrial Marketing*, 14(3), 178–194.

Bengtsson, M. & Kock, S. (2000). "Coopetition" in business networks – to cooperate and compete simultaneously. *Industrial Marketing Management*, 29(5), 411–426.

Bengtsson, M. & Raza-Ullah, T. (2016). A systematic review of research on coopetition: Toward a multilevel understanding. *Industrial Marketing Management*, 57, 23–39.

Bengtsson, M., Wilson, T.L., Bengtsson, M., Eriksson, J. & Wincent, J. (2010). Co-opetition dynamics – an outline for further inquiry. *Competitiveness Review: An International Business Journal*, 20(2), 194–214.

Birkinshaw, J. & Fey, C. (2000). *Building an internal market system: Insights from five R&D organizations*, in Birkinshaw, J. & Hagstrom, P. (eds.) *The flexible firm: Capability management in network organizations*. New York: Oxford University Press.Birkinshaw, J. & Lingblad, M. (2005). Intrafirm competition and charter evolution in a multibusiness firm. *Organization Science*, 16(6), 674–686. Bouncken, R.B., Fredrich, V. & Kraus, S. (2020). Configurations of firm-level value capture in coopetition. *Long Range Planning*, 53(1), 101869.

Bouncken, R.B., Gast, J., Kraus, S. & Bogers, M. (2015). Coopetition: A systematic review, synthesis, and future research directions. *Review of Managerial Science*, 9(3), 577–601.

Bouncken, R.B. & Kraus, S. (2013). Innovation in knowledge-intensive industries: The double-edged sword of coopetition. *Journal of Business Research*, 66(-10), 2060–2070.Brandenburger, A. & Nalebuff, B. (1996). *Co-opetition*. New York: Doubleday.

Cantwell, J. & Mudambi, R. (2005). MNE competence-creating subsidiary mandates. *Strategic Management Journal*, 26(12), 1109–1128.

Carney, M., Gedajlovic, E.R., Heugens, P.P., Van Essen, M. & Van Oosterhout, J. (2011). Business group affiliation, performance, context, and strategy: A meta-analysis. *Academy of Management Journal*, 54(3), 437–460.

Cerrato, D. (2006). The multinational enterprise as an internal market system. *International Business Review*, 15(3), 253–277.

Chambers, M. (2015). *Dynamic inter-subsidiary relationships of competition and collaboration*. Dissertation. Cranfield University.Chang, S.J. & Hong, J. (2000). Economic performance of group-affiliated companies in Korea: Intragroup resource sharing and internal business transactions. *Academy of Management Journal*, 43(3), 429–448.

Chang, S.J. & Hong, J. (2002). How much does the business group matter in Korea? *Strategic Management Journal*, 23(3), 265–274.

Chen, M., Tang, T. Y., Wu, S., & Wang, F. (2020). The double-edged sword of coopetition: differential effects of cross-functional coopetition on product and service innovations. *Journal of Business & Industrial Marketing*, 36(2), 191–202.

Chen, L.J. & Tsou, H.T. (2020). "Of course, cooperation first": The effect of subsidiary capability and perception gaps for subsidiary development. *Multinational Business Review*, 28(3), 401–426.

Chiambaretto, P., Massé, D., & Mirc, N. (2019). "All for One and One for All?"-Knowledge broker roles in managing tensions of internal coopetition: The Ubisoft case. *Research Policy*, 48(3), 584–600.

Chiambaretto, P., Maurice, J. & Willinger, M. (2020). Value creation and value appropriation in innovative coopetition projects. *M@n@gement*, 23(2), 61–75.

Chung, C.N. (2001). Markets, culture and institutions: The emergence of large business groups in Taiwan, 1950s–1970s. *Journal of Management Studies*, 38(5), 719–745.

Ciabuschi, F., Dellestrand, H., & Kappen, P. (2012). The good, the bad, and the ugly: Technology transfer competence, rent-seeking, and bargaining power. *Journal of World Business*, 47(4), 664–674.

Cygler, J., Aluchna, M., Marciszewska, E., Witek-Hajduk, M. & Materna, G. (2012). *Kooperencja przedsiębiorstw w dobie globalizacji. Wyzwania strategiczne, uwarunkowania prawne* [Enterprise coopetition in the age of globalization. Strategic challenges, legal conditions]. Warszawa: Wolters Kluwers Polska.

Cygler, J., Sroka, W., Solesvik, M. & Dębkowska, K. (2018). Benefits and drawbacks of coopetition: The roles of scope and durability in coopetitive relationships. *Sustainability*, 10(8), 2688.

Czakon, W. (2014). *Koopetycja w rozwoju przedsiębiorstw high-tech* [Coopetition in the growth of high-tech enterprises], in Zakrzewska-Bielawska, A. (ed.) *Koopetycja w rozwoju przedsiębiorstw high-tech: Determinanty i dynamika* [Coopetition in the growth of high-tech enterprises: Determinants and dynamics]. Warszawa: Placet.

Czakon, W. & Czernek, K. (2016). The role of trust-building mechanisms in entering into network coopetition: The case of tourism networks in Poland. *Industrial Marketing Management*, 57, 64–74.

Czakon, W. Mucha-Kuś, K. & Rogalski, M. (2014). Coopetition research landscape – A systematic literature review 1997–2010. *Journal of Economics & Management*, 17, 122–150.

Czakon, W., Srivastava, M.K., Le Roy, F. & Gnyawali, D. (2020). Coopetition strategies: Critical issues and research directions. *Long Range Planning*, 53(1), 101948.

Dagnino, G.B. (2009). *Coopetition strategy: A new kind of interfirm dynamics for value creation*, in Dagnino, G.B. & Rocco, E. (eds.) *Coopetition strategy. Theory, experiments and cases*. London: Routledge.

Dagnino, G. & Padula, G. (2002), *Coopetition strategy a new kind of interfirm dynamics for value creation*, EURAM – The European Academy of Management Second Annual Conference "Innovative Research in Management", Stockholm, 9–11 May.

Dal-Soto F. & Monticelli, J. (2017). Coopetition strategies in the Brazilian higher education. *Revista de Administração de Empresas*, 57(1), 65–78.

Dellestrand, H. & Kappen, P. (2012). The effects of spatial and contextual factors on headquarters resource allocation to MNE subsidiaries. *Journal of International Business Studies*, 43(3), 219–243.

Dellestrand, H., Kappen, P. & Lindahl, O. (2020). Headquarter resource allocation strategies and subsidiary competitive or cooperative behavior: Achieving a fit for value creation. *Journal of Organization Design*, 9(1), 1–16.

Devece, C., Ribeiro-Soriano, D.E. & Palacios-Marqués, D. (2019). Coopetition as the new trend in inter-firm alliances: Literature review and research patterns. *Review of Managerial Science*, 13(2), 207–226.

Dorn, S., Schweiger, B. & Albers, S. (2016). Levels, phases and themes of coopetition: A systematic literature review and research agenda. *European Management Journal*, 34, 484–500.

Enright, M.J. & Subramanian, V. (2007). An organizing framework for MNC subsidiary typologies. *Management International Review*, 47(6), 895–924.

Fong, C.M., Ho, H.L., Weng, L.C. & Yang, K.P. (2007). The intersubsidiary competition in an MNE: Evidence from the Greater China region. *Canadian Journal of Administrative Sciences/Revue Canadienne des Sciences de l'Administration*, 24(1), 45–57.

Gernsheimer, O., Kanbach, D.K. & Gast, J. (2021). Coopetition research – a systematic literature review on recent accomplishments and trajectories. *Industrial Marketing Management*, 96, 113–134.

Gnyawali, D.R. & Charleton, R.T. (2018). Nuances in the interplay of competition and cooperation: Towards a theory of coopetition. *Journal of Management*, 44(7), 2511–2534.

Gnyawali, D.R., He, J. & Madhavan, R. (2006). Impact of co-opetition on firm competitive behavior: An empirical examination. *Journal of Management*, 32(4), 507–530.

Gnyawali, D.R. & Park, B.J. (2009). Co-opetition and technological innovation in small and medium-sized enterprises: A multilevel conceptual model. *Journal of Small Business Management*, 47(3), 308–330.

Gopalan, R., Nanda, V. & Seru, A. (2014). Internal capital market and dividend policies: Evidence from business groups. *The Review of Financial Studies*, 27(4), 1102–1142.

Haas, M.R. & Cummings, J.N. (2015). Barriers to knowledge seeking within MNC teams: Which differences matter most? *Journal of International Business Studies*, 46(1), 36–62.

He, J., Mao, X., Rui, O.M. & Zha, X. (2013). Business groups in China. *Journal of Corporate Finance*, 22, 166–192.

Hong, J.F. & Snell, R.S. (2015). Knowledge development through co-opetition: A case study of a Japanese foreign subsidiary and its local suppliers. *Journal of World Business*, 50(4), 769–780.

Hutter, K., Hautz, J., Füller, J., Mueller, J. & Matzler, K. (2011). Communitition: The tension between competition and collaboration in community-based design contests. *Creativity and Innovation Management*, 20(1), 3–21.

Kasper, H. & Mühlbacher, J. (2008). Organizational context and knowledge transfer of a high-tech MNC: A balanced approach to successful European-Asian cooperation. *Chinese Management Studies*, 2(2), 153–163.

Kim, Y. & Lui, S.S. (2015). The impacts of external network and business group on innovation: Do the types of innovation matter? *Journal of Business Research*, 68(9), 1964–1973.

Köseoğlu, M.A., Yildiz, M., Okumus, F. & Barca, M. (2018). The intellectual structure of coopetition: Past, present and future. *Journal of Strategy and Management*, 12(1), 2–29.

Kotzab, H. & Teller, C. (2003). Value-adding partnerships and co-opetition models in the grocery industry. *International Journal of Physical Distribution & Logistics Management*, 33(3), 268–281.

Kylänen, M. & Rusko, R. (2011). Unintentional coopetition in the service industries: The case of Pyhä-Luosto tourism destination in the Finnish Lapland. *European Management Journal*, 29(3), 193–205.

Lagerström, K., Leite, E. & Pahlberg, C. (2021). *Cooperating while competing in multinational corporations*, in Arora-Jonsson, S., Brunsson, N., Hasse, R. & Lagerström, K. (eds.) *Competition: What it is and why it happens.* New York: Oxford University Press.

Le Roy, F. & Czakon, W. (2016). Managing coopetition: The missing link between strategy and performance. *Industrial Marketing Management*, 53(1), 3–6.

Leff, N.H. (1978). Industrial organization and entrepreneurship in the developing countries: The economic groups. *Economic Development and Cultural Change*, 26(4), 661–675.

Liu, Y., Jiao, J. & Xia, J. (2019). Subsidiary networks and foreign subsidiary performance: A coopetition perspective. *Management and Organization Review*, 15(-1), 111–143.

Luo, Y. (2004). A coopetition perspective of MNC–host government relations. *Journal of International Management*, 10(4), 431–451.

Luo, Y. (2005). Toward coopetition within a multinational enterprise: A perspective from foreign subsidiaries. *Journal of World Business*, 40(1), 71–90.

Luo, Y. (2007). A coopetition perspective of global competition. *Journal of World Business*, 42, 129–144.

Luo, X., Slotegraaf, R.J. & Pan. X. (2006). Cross-functional "coopetition": The simultaneous role of cooperation and competition within firms. *Journal of Marketing*, 70, 67–80.

Mierzejewska, W. (2018). Koopetycja w grupach kapitałowych [Coopetition in business groups]. *Studia Ekonomiczne*, 351, 121–130.

Mierzejewska, W. & Dziurski, P. (2021). How firms cooperate in business groups? Evidence from Poland. *Central European Management Journal*, 29(2), 63–88.

Moore, J. & Curry, Sh. (1996). The death of competition. *Fortune*, 133(7), 42–144.

Mudambi, R. (2011). Hierarchy, coordination, and innovation in the multinational enterprise. *Global Strategy Journal*, 1(3-4), 317–323.

Osarenkhoe, A. (2010). A coopetition strategy – a study of inter-firm dynamics between competition and cooperation. *Business Strategy Series*, 11(6), 343–362.

Park, B.J.R., Srivastava, M.K. & Gnyawali, D.R. (2014). Walking the tight rope of coopetition: Impact of competition and cooperation intensities and balance on firm innovation performance. *Industrial Marketing Management*, 43(2), 210–221.

Peng, T.J.A. & Bourne, M. (2009). The coexistence of competition and cooperation between networks: Implications from two Taiwanese healthcare networks. *British Journal of Management*, 20(3), 377–400.

Porter, M.E. (1985). *Competitive advantage: Creating and sustaining superior performance.* New York: Free Press.

Ricciardi, F., Zardini, A., Czakon, W., Rossignoli, C. & Kraus, S. (2021). Revisiting the cooperation–competition paradox: A configurational approach to short-and long-term coopetition performance in business networks. *European Management Journal,* in press.

Ritala, P. (2012). Coopetition strategy–when is it successful? Empirical evidence on innovation and market performance. *British Journal of Management*, 23(3), 307–324.

Ritala, P., Golnam, A. & Wegmann, A. (2014). Coopetition-based business models: The case of Amazon. com. *Industrial Marketing Management*, 43(2), 236–249.

Robert, M., Chiambaretto, P., Mira, B. & Le Roy, F. (2018). Better, faster, stronger, the impact of market oriented coopetition on product commercial performance. *M@n@gement*, 21(1), 574–610.

Rugman, A.M. & Verbeke, A. (2001). Subsidiary-specific advantages in multinational enterprises. *Strategic Management Journal*, 22(3), 237–250.

Santos, J.N. (2021). Linking joint value creation to the interplay of competition and cooperation: A fuzzy set approach. *Industrial Marketing Management*, 92, 45–54.

Schleimer, S. & Riege, A. (2009). Knowledge transfer between globally dispersed units at BMW. *Journal of Knowledge Management*, 3(1), 27–41.

Schmid, S. & Maurer, J. (2011). *Relationships between MNC subsidiaries–Opening a black box in the international business field*, in Schmidt, S. (ed.) *Internationale Unternehmungen und das Management ausländischer Tochtergesellschaften.* Wiesbaden: Gabler.

Song, J., Lee, K. & Khanna, T. (2016). Dynamic capabilities at Samsung: Optimizing internal co-opetition. *California Management Review*, 58(4), 118–140.

Tidström, A. (2014). Managing tensions in coopetition. *Industrial Marketing Management*, 43(2), 261–271.

Tippmann, E., Scott, P.S., Reilly, M. & O'Brien, D. (2018). Subsidiary coopetition competence: Navigating subsidiary evolution in the multinational corporation. *Journal of World Business*, 53(4), 540–554.

Tippmann, E., Sharkey Scott, P. & Parker, A. (2017). Boundary capabilities in MNCs: Knowledge transformation for creative solution development. *Journal of Management Studies*, 54(4), 455–482.

Tsai, K.H. & Hsu, T.T. (2014). Cross-functional collaboration, competitive intensity, knowledge integration mechanisms, and new product performance: A mediated moderation model. *Industrial Marketing Management*, 43(2), 293–303.

Tsai, W. (2002). Social structure of "coopetition" within a multiunit organization: Coordination, competition, and intraorganizational knowledge sharing. *Organization Science*, 13(2), 179–190.

Yami S., Castaldo S., Dagnino G., Le Roy F. & Czakon W. (2010), Introduction-*coopetition strategies: Toward a new form of inter-organizational dynamics?* in Yami S., Castaldo S., Dagnino G. & Le Roy F. (eds.) *Coopetition: Winning strategies for the 21st century.* Cheltenham and Northampton: Edward Elgar Publishing Limited.

Yiu, D., Bruton, G.D. & Lu, Y. (2005). Understanding business group performance in an emerging economy: Acquiring resources and capabilities in order to prosper. *Journal of Management Studies*, 42(1), 183–206.

Zakrzewska-Bielawska, A. (2013). *Coopetition in high-technology firms: Resource-based determinantsi*, in Zaharim A. & Rodrigues R.G. (eds.) *Recent advances in management, marketing and finances.* Business and Economic Series, 4, 51–56.

Zhang, F., Jiang, G. & Cantwell, J.A. (2019). Geographically dispersed technological capability building and MNC innovative performance: The role of intra-firm flows of newly absorbed knowledge. *Journal of International Management*, 25(3), 100669.

Zona, F., Boyd, B.K. & Haynes, K.T. (2019). Coordination, control, or charade? The role of board interlocks among business group members. *Management Decision*, 57(10), 2630–2652.

3 Coopetitive Tensions within Business Groups

Anna Krejner-Nowecka

Introduction

Coopetition management is often examined as an organisational phenomenon (Nalebuff & Brandenburger, 1997; Bengtsson & Raza-Ullah, 2016). The amount of literature on coopetition is enormous. Despite this attention, research findings are often contradictory, inconclusive, and incomplete. Throughout this book, it is demonstrated that multilevel influences shape coopetition policies and practices. In a multilevel framework, understanding parameters of coopetition requires investigating dynamics and effects at firm, group, organisational, and individual levels (Fernandez et al., 2014; Le Roy & Fernandez, 2015; Gnyawali et al., 2016). Intrafirm level coopetition between subunits, groups, or teams within one entity (such as an organisation or business group) has a different nature and dynamics due to the power distribution influencing the intrafirm relationship (Bendig et al., 2018). There are only a few studies that investigate the coopetition within business groups (Tsai, 2002; Luo et al., 2006; Aluchna, 2013; Mierzejewska, 2018; Dziurski, 2020).

The recent focus of coopetition studies has shifted from firm level to a network level of analysis (Bengtsson & Kock, 2014), but the missing component in coopetition studies is still individuals (employees, managers, or entrepreneurial founders), who participate in and make sense of coopetition strategies (Galkina & Lundgren-Henriksson, 2017; Czakon et al., 2020). Especially managers as professional workers and agents of organisational change are the most visible, if not the most effective players in the process of managing coopetition within business groups due to their professed role in the design and implementation of coopetition processes. This chapter examines the nature of tensions in business groups with hope to better understand the role of leaders and the way in which they can contribute to managing coopetition. It focuses solely on the analysis of the aspects of simultaneous cooperation and competition linked to conflicts and methods of conflict management. This particular focus provides an insight related to the emotional management of organisational paradoxes during coopetition, while acknowledging that other factors (juridical and structural solutions) also influence the coopetitive process. By combining the

DOI: 10.4324/9781003324775-4

understanding of a business group phenomenon with that of the paradox literature, it expands understanding of why, how, and when contradictory goals and multiple partners' expectations result in tensions and how these tensions can be managed.

Theoretical Lenses

Tensions in Coopetition

Coopetition within business groups is still a new research objective that has been emerging in business practice around the world. Prior empirical research has explored the positive impact of coopetition on firms (performance-enhancing benefits) (Ritala, 2012; Crick, 2018), but there are prominent drawbacks, such as the potential risk of collaborating with untrustworthy rivals that exploit their partners for opportunistic gains (Raza-Ullah et al., 2014; Yan et al., 2020; Crick & Crick, 2021). Coopetition may contribute to improving players' performance but also creates instability and tensions that may occur not only between two parties but among all those parties involved (Le Roy & Fernandez, 2015).

Tension is a psychological and behavioural phenomenon but has been used interchangeably in the business literature to describe conflict. The meaning of tension for some authors is like the meaning of conflict, competition, burden, crises, and problem (Tidström, 2014). The meta-theory that offers a lens through which a tension can be understood is the paradox theory. It is formally defined by Smith and Lewis (2011) giving the basis to related concepts such as tensions, contradictions, dilemmas, and dialectics (Putnam et al., 2016; Schad et al., 2016). As paradox, tensions represent contradictory viewpoints or intentions and are described in terms of relational and transactional exchanges, differences in time horizons between emergent and strategic orientations, and contradictions between trust and competition (Quinton & Wilson, 2016).

The first attempt to employ cognitive and emotive dimensions in analyses of coopetition tensions is an article by Raza-Ullah et al. (2014). In the early stages of coopetition, structural, legal, and contractual challenges typically occur; however, as the cooperative relationship develops, tensions can also be experienced emotionally. Since emotions – positive (e.g. happiness and excitement) and negative (e.g. sadness and anger) – influence human cognition, communication, and behaviour, they can also influence the processing of complex information, making quality decisions and performance outcomes in coopetitive relationships (Huy, 2011; Vuori & Huy, 2020; Hagelin & Sætre, 2021).

The most common tensions in coopetition are related to both creating and appropriating value (Ritala & Tidstrom, 2014), both sharing knowledge and protecting knowledge (Jarvenpaa & Majchrzak, 2016), both learning from each other and winning the learning race, and both getting close and keeping a distance (Raza-Ullah, 2017). It might be role conflicts, power, and dependence, as well as opportunism, which in practice may occur simultaneously (Tidström, 2014). Role-conflicts can be found at firm or individual level. Having different opinions about the degree and type of responsibilities creates tensions between goals. Knowledge sharing is an important objective in coopetition, as it adds value to each organisation (Chin et al., 2008). Another type of tension in coopetitive relationships relates to a lack of balance in power and dependence. A study by Jehn and Mannix (2001) adds the following tensions: relationship conflicts with affective components (i.e. emotional differences) and personal issues (i.e. incompatible value systems), task conflicts (related to cognitive components), or process conflicts.

Tensions are often linked to conflicts and are even used interchangeably in the literature. There are several approaches to types of organisational conflicts, but in the study, two dimensions are examined – one consisting of disagreements relating to the task or other business-related issues (substantive conflict) and other concerned with the feelings or emotions of the conflicting parties involved in such a situation (affective conflict) (Jehn, 1994).

Affective/interpersonal/people-to-people causes come from personal characters when people interact. As noted by Deutsch and Coleman (2006), the existence of affective conflicts is always the resultant of several factors coinciding, among which they enumerate individuals' subjectivism in their understanding and sense of social justice, unsatisfied needs and the motivation arising from them, the lack of sufficient communication between the parties, difficulties controlling one's own emotions when facing difficulties or the unknown, the aspiration for greater power, desire to take out negative emotions (aggression), personality traits predisposing one to specific behaviours (personality), impact of culture and worldview on ways of reception, and interpretation of meanings contained in the communication process. Since there exists no social configuration free of disputes or conflicts, it is only natural for conflicts to arise from interpersonal differences.

Substantive/organisational causes of conflict are consequence of the characteristics of organisational design, limited resources and characteristics of organisational systems, differentiation of organisational units, and incompatibility of operating goals. A stream of literature has also discussed the following causes: social (the struggle for agency or power), psychological (a feeling of personal conflict), and tactical conflict (a conscious choice) in a political context (Fang et al., 2011).

Tensions and conflicts can be managed, but it is important to recognise both the style of management and the nature of the relationship conflicts (underlying issues). Moreover, the various forms of tensions management produce different kinds of outcomes, which can be negative (termination of the relationship between firms), positive (new ideas and methods), or mixed (both positive and negative). According to Tidstrom (2014), as several types of tensions are evident in different types of coopetition, it might be possible to predict these tensions, but all outcomes are positive for at least one of the parties. The goals of the coopetition between competitors may influence the choice of management style.

Managing Critical Tensions through Functional Leadership Behaviour

Theoretical and empirical studies of organisational paradoxes (Smith & Lewis, 2011) conclude that in coopetitive relationships (similarly as in ambidextrous firms) the critical issue is not to minimise tensions, but rather to manage it for the beneficial outcomes of coopetition to be realised. Mariani (2016) suggests that coordination mechanisms with varying degrees of formality seem to play a crucial role to manage coopetitive interactions.

A firm's capacity to manage cooperative and competitive tensions is crucial for the emergence of synergies (Hill & Jones, 1992), and a question arises about how to do so. Several researchers have pointed to the importance of leadership, development of trust, and long-term commitment as the most important factors for coopetition success (Bengtsson et al., 2016; Bouncken et al., 2016; Vanyushyn et al., 2017). By setting the direction of change, leaders play a crucial role in determining the strategic direction of an organisation and therefore have a substantial bearing on organisational outcomes (Kotter, 2001). According to the leadership contingency theory (Fiedler, 1964) and the functional leadership theory (Fleishman et al., 1991; Morgeson et al., 2010), leadership is expected to occur along two key dimensions: task performance and relationship orientation. Nesse (2018) stresses especially functional leadership behaviours, because coopetition is not an easy strategy to manage. The emotional-relational dimension relates to how leaders deal with paradoxical tensions and emotional ambivalence that sustain the coopetitive relationship, while the task-performance dimension embodies functional leadership behaviours characterised as problem-solving or goal-oriented activities that are conscious actions or tasks performed by individual leaders to achieve desired outcomes of a project.

In a business group, tensions and their level are also linked to the level of decision-making autonomy afforded to subsidiaries. Remaining under uniform management can translate into a restriction of the entrepreneurial decision-making freedom on the highest tier of leadership within each individual business group affiliate. Furthermore, there exist internal ties of personal, economic, and legal nature between the parent company and subsidiaries as well as among the subsidiaries themselves. This leads not only to high commonalities but also to smaller opportunism risks. Concentration of decision-making powers in the parent company often means that the subsidiaries lack decision-making autonomy. Instead, they have a defined scope of decision-making powers permitting them to execute their current tasks arising from the whole business group's policy. Accordingly, a lack of tension at the top tier may be the result of the scope of decision-making authority (the power to make choices), the level of decision-making autonomy, and, lastly, the decision-making leeway.[1]

Recently, it has been highlighted that handling – rather than acceptance – of tension is more relevant. In the handling of tension, and opposed to the dyadic relationship, a single party cannot easily disconnect from all its network parties, and the network contextualises the dynamics of tension (Oberg et al., 2020), which may "move" around the network as initial tension is dealt with.

Much of the existing research on tensions relies on research on Thomas and Kilmann's (1974) model of conflict management with its five conflict handling styles: competition, avoidance, compromise, accommodation, and collaboration. The five approaches range in levels of the one group's attempt to satisfy personal concerns (assertiveness), and their attempt to satisfy the concerns of others (cooperativeness). Thomas and Kilmann's grid shows some conflict management styles focus on maintaining the relationship between the parties involved at the expense of the outcome while others prioritise the outcome over relationships. However, such conflict management styles (as presented in the original models) do not seem to fit coopetitive business relationships (e.g. the compromise style seems not to fit unless similarity within a cooperative business relationship exists). In business group settings, the parent company concurrently plays the double role of decision-maker, by reducing the opportunistic behaviour of divisions due to their control and mediation of conflicts, and of "go-between" by encouraging and facilitating coopetitive interaction between divisions to prevent the waste of resources and achieve economies of scale (Mariani, 2009; Czakon & Czernek, 2016; Amata et al., 2022). On the other hand, in coopetition, especially in situations with high competition and low cooperation (inbuilt tension between individualism and sharing), the most common strategies are avoidance and competition, which result in mixed outcomes, implying both positive and negative perceptions. The findings show that in comparison with other managing methods, collaboration produces a positive outcome for all parties although its adoption might be more challenging in forced and highly competitive relationships (Tidström, 2014).

Padula and Dagnino (2021) examine how the reciprocal dependence in coopetition both generates and weakens tensions in relation to the actions taken intended to benefit both firms. Focusing on tensions in networks, it can be handled through coalition, decreased engagement/withdrawal, diffusion, and confrontation, where all but the coalition style leads to new tensions. Coalition indicates how the strengthening of ties and increased trust lessens the risk for tensions, while the pooling of interests and the alliancing with other parties increase the risk for continuous tensions.

Consequences of handling tensions create new tensions in the current relationships (imploding) or in new ones (exploding) (Minà & Dagnino, 2021).

Raza-Ullah (2020) suggests that entities with different – even conflicting – goals, cultural values, and operational routines can be managed through organisational-level mechanisms, namely, emotional and balancing capabilities. Multiple, complex, and inconsistent emotions of managers can be regulated through antecedent-focused (change the appraisal, avoid information) or response-focused mechanisms (control or suppress one's later emotions) (Schutte et al., 2009; Ashforth et. al., 2014). Such capability is thus a must-have competence of top managers. To do two opposing things simultaneously, the manager must be highly motivated to explore and exploit activities and opportunities (Tushman & O'Reilly, 1996).

Not only conflict management styles make a difference in coopetition relationship, but also the mindsets of management, risk appetites, and people skills may be the determining factor for success. Being a manager in coopetitive settings requires a dramatic change in mindset. In the literature, one can find a list of antecedents: cooperative orientation, experience in coopetition, participation in existing networks, perceived benefits, partner's reputation, trust in partners, and strategic fit (Staniec & Zakrzewska-Bielawska, 2020). Directly unmeasurable and unobservable coopetition antecedents may be reflected in specific, observable behaviours (e.g. formal and social relationships within networks), attitudes (e.g. manifested trust in coopetitors, acknowledged reputation of the competitor, and cooperative orientation), perceived states (e.g. strategic fit in terms of resources), or conditions (e.g. mutually perceived and taken benefits).

Results from the research of Seepana et al. (2020) offer three important implications for managers of firms that engage in coopetition:

1 To maintain strong knowledge-sharing routines with their partners as such routines can complement the effect of their firm's strategic intent.
2 Managers need to possess ambidextrous skills of simultaneous exploration and exploitation when engaging in strategic alliances such as coopetition.
3 It is important for managers to ensure the use of both ambidextrous skills and knowledge sharing routines concurrently to assist their firms in pursuing successful coopetition.

Leading a change in organisational dynamics starts inside managers' heads. Behavioural theories indicate the existence of differences in decision-making at the individual level due to personality type, so the interpretation and application of managerial roles are primarily influenced by the individual's intentions. Traditionally at the organisational level, when the parties have a common interest in achieving their goals, they undertake cooperation activities. In the opposite situation, when the implementation of the goals of one-party conflicts with the interests of the other party, they are dealing with competition. In todays networked world, where relationships between companies are more and more complex, the approach to rivals is also changing, and hence the mindset and style of managing.

To manage the paradox and tension in coopetition relationship Raza-Ullah (2017) proposes that firm's leadership could include three main components – analytical, emotional, and balancing. The analytical dimension highlights the importance of senior manager's mindset and managers' ability to think paradoxically, to explore the tension in a creative way that captures both extremes rather than focusing either on the cooperative or competitive dimensions of coopetition (Eisenhardt & Marti, 2000; Smith & Tushman, 2005; Raza-Ullah, 2018). Managers equally predisposed to intragroup competition and cooperation tend to be developing a clear, precise, and unified understanding of paradoxical situation, constantly scan the business environment, assess potential opportunities and threats, and identify if there is a need to cooperate with competitor (Raza-Ullah, 2018). The balancing dimension of coopetition refers to the ability of managers to develop routines and processes that enable and foster the separation, integration, and balance of contradictory forces. The emotional dimension of coopetition refers to the ability of managers to accept, understand, and regulate ambivalent emotions and their effects (Raza-Ullah, 2017).

Managers envisioning, at the same time, both cooperation and competition as a "conceptual model of thinking" and interpreting it as a "predictable business process", offer specific "decision enablers" solutions in contradictory goals and multiple partners expectations. Coopetitive mindset is not only critical but also delivers better business groups outcomes. Such managers do not see the future as a negative one, but as an opportunity to growth, and they better manage a rising tensions.

Scholars call for future research to investigate the nature of ambidextrous managers in coopetitive relationships (Czakon et al., 2019, Felício et al., 2019) and suggest that the adoption of a relational approach to understanding leadership could be promising.

Empirical Findings

The study, which results are presented in the chapter, uses a survey database of 121 business groups in Poland that was drawn from the databases of business groups that a parent company is listed on the Warsaw Stock Exchange. Data were acquired from surveys with top managers of parent companies from randomly selected business groups, Amadeus database and financial statements published by business groups. Information about the research sample and method is presented in the introduction. This chapter examines the nature of tensions in business groups with hope to better understand the role of leaders and the way in which they can contribute to managing coopetition.

Table 3.1 Coopetition skill assessment of managers in business groups

	Frequency	*Percentage*
Clearly predisposed to intragroup competition	0	0
Tend to be predisposed to intragroup competition	13	10.7
Equally predisposed to intragroup competition and cooperation	74	61.2
They tend to be predisposed to intragroup cooperation	15	12.4
Clearly predisposed to intragroup cooperation	19	15.7
Total	121	100.0

Source: Own elaboration.

It is important for managers to recognise, analyse, and accept their management style. Thus, the study firstly assesses the coopetition skills of managers in business groups studied (Table 3.1).

Managers in business groups studied strongly declare simultaneously having predispositions for cooperation and competition. A total of 61.2% of respondents emphasise that they are ready and able to both compete and collaborate within a business group. Furthermore, 10.7% of respondents state that they have predispositions to activities related to competition, 12.4% that they are rather predisposed to cooperation in a coopetition relationship within a business group, and 15.7% that they clearly have predispositions to activities related to cooperation. This is in line with the previous literature findings showing the dilemma between sharing and protecting in business groups under the common management is not so critical as in the other settings. In the case of coopetition, firms serve strategic targets which require the development of formal planning procedures (March & Simon, 1958; Armstrong 1982) and provide guidance to those dealing with coopetition. Clear parent company expectations help subsidiaries adapt their behaviour and develop coopetition specific routines. A formal coopetition strategy provides goals, aspiration levels, and behavioural guidance and helps managers find the way through multiple contradictions and competitive tensions in coopetition (Bengtsson et al., 2016; Tidstrom & Rajala, 2016; Bouncken et al., 2020). On the other hand, 10.7% of respondents argue that they are rather predisposed to activities related to competition in business group relations.

The above summary of the percentage of indications of cooperation, competition, and coexistence of cooperation and competition skills possess by managers of business groups at the parent company level shows a tendency for high ratings for cooperation compared to competition but also the readiness for simultaneous cooperation and competition.

How do leaders manage paradoxical tensions in the context of coopetition depends on the character of them. Findings show (Table 3.2) that managers during coopetition within business groups frequently deal with substantive than interpersonal conflicts.

Table 3.2 The existence of affective/interpersonal/people-to-people conflicts

Existence of (inter)personal conflicts	*Frequency*	*Percentage*
Yes	33	27.3
No	87	71.9
Not sure	1	0.8
Total	121	100.0

Source: Own elaboration.

In most business groups studied (71.9%), respondents do not find personal conflicts to exist. It is surmised that this can be linked to the existence of personal ties in the business group structure (equity, management, or employment ties). Especially, management ties occurring in a combination of roles in the various bodies of a business group's companies (executive or supervisory boards) referred to as a personal union (management union) have a significant impact on the organisational and social cohesion of a business group. It must be noted that a personal union in the sense of an organisational solution defines formal personal ties in business groups, whereas personal bonds originate primarily from social relations. The emergence of personal bonds depends strongly on the organisational culture, trust, and loyalty within a business group's organisational and social structure. Nonetheless, 27.3% of respondents indicate the existence of conflicts of interpersonal nature.

Another matter analysed in the study is the existence of substantively based conflicts in a mutual relationship of cooperation and competition at the highest tier, i.e. involving the selection of goals, tasks, and processes (Table 3.3).

The literature notes that belonging to a business group affects the cooperating companies' attitudes and behaviours, determining their engagement in cooperation and communication, as well as being conducive to tensions (conflicts). More substantive tensions (62.8%) than interpersonal ones (27.3%) are observed. Beliefs relating to substantively based tensions (conflicts) differ significantly, with 36.4% of the respondents believing them not to exist and 62.8% perceiving them in relationships at the highest leadership tier of business groups.

Although coopetition within business group tends to be beneficial, a coopetitive relationship can be difficult to sustain and balance as tensions often are connected to difficulty of working together (interpersonal conflicts). The explanation on how leaders manage the paradoxical tensions in coopetition relations might depend on the type of conflicts, are they interpersonal or substantive. Leaders need not only structural and legal framework but also cognitive behaviours to handle and control their emotions to increase performance.

Table 3.3 The existence of substantive conflicts on highest tiers of leadership

Existence of substantive conflicts	*Frequency*	*Percentage*
Yes	76	62.8
No	44	36.4
Nor sure	1	0.8
Total	121	100.0

Source: Own elaboration.

Table 3.4 Managers' way of dealing with tensions arising from coopetition

When tensions arise	*Frequency*	*Percentage*
Tend to cooperate	112	92.6
Avoidance/frustration	9	7.4
Total	121	100.0

Source: Own elaboration.

It is necessary to recall that the primary goal of creation and management of a business group is cooperation, which means the orientation of all companies therein to the achievement of not only their individual goals but above all the goals of the whole business group. Additionally, the company's size and age will set specific conditions for value capture in coopetition (Gnyawali & Park, 2009; Robert et al., 2009). Hence, the study assumes that, faced with tensions (conflicts), managers of parent companies would decisively more often tend to cooperate to overcome such difficulties. The results of the analyses are presented in Table 3.4.

92.6% of respondents argue that coopetition relationships within studied business groups are characterised by a prevalent tendency to cooperate to deal with rising tensions, which is consistent with reasons for creating business groups as well as related situation in which the highest tier of managers of the parent company decides the direction of actions taken by the subsidiaries. In a situation in which companies from a business group make their own voluntary choice, one can observe fewer difficulties with coordination (issuing of instructions), easier information flow, awareness of own competence limits, and sense of responsibility. In effect, competitive behaviours manifesting as frustration are far less frequent. Moreover, frustration-related behaviours may arise from managers' belief of being better at taking advantage of opportunities (Bouncken & Fredrich, 2016). In subsidiaries, high-level experience might be in a negative relation to a formal strategy. As Bouncken et al. (2015) put it, the level of competitive behaviour and perceived competitive behaviour change within a coopetition arrangement over time (Chen et al., 2007; Giachetti & Dagnino, 2014). Managers might act more or less competitively when specific intermediate targets are or are not met. The actual and perceived competitive behaviour might change during a project and force managers into more or less opportunistic value capture behaviour.

It must be noted that a tendency to cooperate may require a constructive approach to conflict resolution, which is one of the most desirable methods but also one of the most difficult, for it presupposes having certain competence and the ability to understand the very essence of the conflict and to make the right decisions in conflict resolution. Among others, such skills include the ability to establish a working relationship between parties (mediation), creation of a safe and friendly atmosphere (prenegotiation), active listening and communication based on the parties' needs and positions, identification of common goals, realisation of mistakes, development of standards, and progress monitoring with simultaneous care to maintain the group's cohesion. Identification and diagnosis of the nature of the problem as it arises, development of possible solutions satisfactory to parties (selection of criteria), and implementation of solutions are all important.

Conclusion

This study examines tensions in the coopetition relationship context of business groups. Coopetitive relationships can increase innovation and entrepreneurship (Le Roy & Czakon, 2015) but require decreasing tensions around value creation and appropriation (Bouncken et al., 2018). Managing critical tensions through functional leadership behaviour could improve the transfer of ideas, knowledge, and resources within subsidiaries of business groups.

In this study, it is assumed that in coopetition relationships, tensions develop and need to be managed. The results indicate that many business group managers appear to agree with this assumption. Additionally, in the opinion of managers, they have a balance between the needed qualities – to cooperate and to compete. The separation of managers' predispositions into two mutually exclusive activities related to competition or cooperation seems inappropriate in a business group setting. It is likely that managers who in a business group incorporate coopetition mindset into their mental programming, with the parent company in mind, are in a better position to capture value from coopetition. They seek to process, integrate, and co-ordinate thoughts to generate synergy and a responsive system that enhances common understanding and interaction. Results also show that in a situation of tension resulting from cooperation and competition at the same time, managers prefer cooperation rather than avoidance or frustration. While the subsidiaries work together, they can share resources and knowledge for value creation and appropriation. Simultaneously, they compete for fair input–output ratios and for value appropriation. Research shows that in the relationship of cooperation and competition between subsidiaries within business groups, there are no conflicts of an interpersonal nature at top management level. On the other hand, substantive conflicts occur much more often. Tensions are related to the choice of goals, implementation of tasks, and processes.

Today's researchers view the prevailing notion in the management literature about putting the micro in macro (Johnson et al., 2003) as adequate for analysing tensions in a coopetition relationship. So, for managers, major changes take place on a business group level, and subsidiaries are not a separate stage but an integral element of an integrated system. In addition, there is a need to move from placing more emphasis on the "successful" qualities for coopetitive managers to highlighting qualities of competent managers. In asserting the qualities needed for success in coopetition, researchers and practitioners alike were concerned with managers' ability to cope with difficulties. Success is often measured in performance-enhancing benefits but ignored the qualitative aspects of relationships with people. This brings a need for competent managers, who can deal effectively with tensions concentrating more on cooperation than frustration to sustain relationships among participating companies, and foster innovation.

The study contains a few limitations restricting the ability to make inferences. The foremost limitation appears to be the fact that the coopetitive relationship is considered only from one side that of the parent company's managers. The ability to understand relationships requires the study of beliefs of all parties involved, followed by in-depth qualitative analyses aimed to facilitate the understanding of intraorganisational tensions and methods of managing (coping with) them or the emergence of causation chains among analysed variables. It is, however, worth observing that the study has opened important fields for research. Both the coopetitive relationships themselves and their various contingencies are complicated, but the study of selected elements of attitudes of persons responsible for coopetition within business groups, the general beliefs concerning the coopetition skills possessed, and the inclination towards specific behaviours when faced with tensions (either cooperation or avoidance) provides insights into certain aspects of behavioural circumstances relating to the quality of coopetition relationships within business groups, the nature of which remains to be explained by future analyses. There is a universal consensus in the literature that to make sure that a relationship is successful one must understand the values, expectations, and motivations of the persons involved in it and especially the managers responsible for the decision-making process. Future research might, therefore, choose a purposeful multiple-case study sampling approach (Anteby et al., 2014) that helps to dig deeper into micro-aspects of managing tensions. Purposeful sampling (Patton, 2002) allows to build a sample capable of providing an in-depth understanding of a specific phenomenon by ensuring richness of information.

Note

1 Decision-making powers must be distinguished conceptually from decision-making autonomy and decision-making leeway. The limitation of managers' decision-making leeway is gradable. Large restrictions occur in the case of decision-making powers (conditioned by the will of the party assigning the permissions), medium restrictions are the case with decision-making autonomy, and small ones when the manager has decision-making leeway (full authority with mainly legal, political, social, or technological limitations).

References

Aluchna, M. (2013). *Kooperencja w grupach kapitałowych kapitałowych* [Coopetition in business groups], in: Cygler, J., Aluchna, M., Marciszewska, E., Witek-Hajduk, M. & Materna, G. (eds.) *Kooperencja przedsiębiorstw w dobie globalizacji. Wyzwania strategiczne, uwarunkowania prawne [Enterprise coopetition in the age of globaliaation. Strategic challenges, legal conditions].* Warszawa: Wolters Kluwers Polska.

Amata, R., Dagnino, G.B., Minà, A. & Picone, P.M. (2022). Managing coopetition in diversified firms: Insights from a qualitative case study. *Long Range Planning*, 55(4), 102128.

Anteby, M., Lifshitz, H. & Tushman, M. (2014). *Using qualitative research for "how" questions*, https://www.strategicmanagement.net/pdfs/qualitative-research-in-strategic-management.pdf (Accessed: 23 February 2017).

Armstrong, J.S. (1982). The value of formal planning for strategic decisions: Review of empirical research. *Strategic Management Journal*, 3(3), 197–211.

Ashforth, B.E., Rogers, K.M., Pratt, M.G. & Pradies, C. (2014). Ambivalence in organizations: A multilevel approach. *Organization Science*, 25(5), 1453–1478.

Bendig, D., Enkeb, S., Thiemea, N. & Brettel, M. (2018). Performance implications of cross-functional coopetition in new product development: The mediating role of organizational learning. *Industrial Marketing Management*, 73, 137–153.

Bengtsson, M. & Kock, S. (2014). Coopetition - Quo vadis? Past accomplishments and future challenges. *Industrial Marketing Management*, 43(2), 180–188.

Bengtsson, M., Kock, S., Lundgren-Henriksson, E.-L. & Nasholm, M.H. (2016). Coopetition research in theory and practice: Growing new theoretical, empirical, and methodological domains. *Industrial Marketing Management*, 57(1), 4–11.

Bengtsson, M. & Raza-Ullah, T. (2016). A systematic review of research on coopetition: Toward a multilevel understanding. *Industrial Marketing Management*, 57, 23–39.

Bouncken, R.B., Clauß, T. & Fredrich, V. (2016). Product innovation through coopetition in alliances: Singular or plural governance? *Industrial Marketing Management*, 53, 77–90.

Bouncken, R.B. & Fredrich, V. (2016). Learning in coopetition: Alliance orientation, network size, and firm types. *Journal of Business Research*, 69(5), 1753–1758.

Bouncken, R.B., Fredrich, V. & Kraus, S. (2020). Configurations of firm-level value capture in coopetition. *Long Range Planning*, 53(1), 101869.

Bouncken, R.B., Fredrich, V., Ritala, P. & Kraus, S. (2018). Coopetition in new product development alliances: Advantages and tensions for incremental and radical innovation. *British Journal of Management*, 29, 391–410.

Bouncken, R.B., Gast, J., Kraus, S. & Bogers, M. (2015). Coopetition: A systematic review, synthesis, and future research directions. *Review of Managerial Science*, 9(3), 577–601.

Chen, L., Lesmond, D.A. & Wei, J. (2007). Corporate yield spreads and bond liquidity. *The Journal of Finance*, 62(1), 119–149.

Chin, K., Chan, B.L. & Lam, P. (2008). Identifying and prioritizing critical success factors for coopetition strategy. *Industrial Management & Data Systems*, 108(4), 437–454.

Crick, J.M. (2018). The facets, antecedents and consequences of coopetition: An entrepreneurial marketing perspective. *Qualitative Market Research*, 21(2), 253–272.Crick, J.M. & Crick, D. (2021). The yin and yang nature of coopetition activities: Non-linear effects and the moderating role of competitive intensity for internationalised firms. *International Marketing Review*, 38(4), 690–716.

Czakon, W. & Czernek, K. (2016). The role of trust-building mechanisms in entering into network coopetition: The case of tourism networks in Poland. *Industrial Marketing Management*, 57(2), 64–74.

Czakon, W., Klimas, P. & Mariani, M. (2020). Behavioral antecedents of coopetition: A synthesis and measurement scale. *Long Range Planning*, 53(1), 101875.

Czakon, W., Srivastava, M.K., Le Roy, F. & Gnyawali, D.R. (2020). Coopetition strategies: Critical issues and research directions. *Long Range Planning*, 53(1), 101948.

Deutsch, M., Coleman, P.T. & Marcus, E.C., (2006). *The handbook of conflict resolution: Theory & practice*. San Francisco, CA: Jossey-Bass.

Dziurski, P. (2020). Interplay between coopetition and innovation: Systematic literature review. *Organization and Management*, 1(188), 9–20.

Eisenhardt, K.M. & Marti, J.A. (2000). Dynamic capabilities: What are they? *Strategic Management Journal*, 21(10–11), 1105–1121.

Fang, S.-R., Fang, S.-C., Chou, C.-H., Yang, S.-M. & Tsai, F.-S. (2011). Relationship learning and innovation: The role of relationship-specific memory. *Industrial Marketing Management*, 40(5), 743–753.

Felício, J.A., Caldeirinha, V. & Dutra, A. (2019). Ambidextrous capacity in small and medium-sized enterprises. *Journal of Business Research*, 101, 607–614.

Fernandez, A.-S., Le Roy, F., & Gnyawali, D. (2014). Sources and management of tension in coopetition case evidence from telecommunications satellites manufacturing in Europe. *Industrial Marketing Management*, 43, 222–235.

Fiedler, F.E. (1964). A contingency model of leadership effectiveness. *Advances in Experimental Social Psychology*, 1, 149–190.

Fleishman, E.A., Zaccaro, S.J. & Mumford, M.D. (1991). Individual differences and leadership: An overview. *The Leadership Quarterly*, 2(4), 237–243.

Galkina, T. & Lundgren-Henriksson, E-L. (2017). Coopetition as an entrepreneurial process: Interplay of causation and effectuation. *Industrial Marketing Management*, 67, 158–173.

Giachetti, C. & Dagnino, G. B. (2014). Detecting the relationship between competitive intensity and firm product line length: Evidence from the worldwide mobile phone industry. *Strategic Management Journal*, 35(9), 1398–1409.

Gnyawali, D.R., Madhavan, R., He, J. & Bengtsson, M. (2016). Sources and management of tension in co-opetition case evidence from telecommunications satellites manufacturing in Europe. *Industrial Marketing Management*, 53, 7–18.

Gnyawali, D.R. & Park, R. (2009). Co-opetition and technological innovation in small and medium-sized enterprises: A multilevel conceptual model. *Journal of Small Business Management*, 47, 308–330.

Hagelin, J.G. & Sætre, S.H. (2021). *The functions of leadership in managing paradoxical tensions in coopetitive interfirm strategies: A qualitative case study from the Fintech industry.* Master Thesis. Norwegian School of Economics, Bergen.

Hill, Ch. W.L. & Jones, T.M. (1992). Stakeholder-agency theory. *Journal of Management Studies*, 29(2), 131–154.

Huy, Q.N. (2011). How middle managers' group focus emotions and social identities influence strategy implementation. *Strategic Management Journal*, 32, 1387–1410.

Jarvenpaa, S. & Majchrzak, A. (2016). Interactive self-regulatory theory for sharing and protecting in inter-organizational collaborations. *Academy of Management Review*, 41(1), 1–19.

Jehn, K.A. (1994). Enhancing effectiveness: An investigation of advantages and disadvantages of value-based intragroup conflict. *International Journal of Conflict Management*, 5, 223–238.

Jehn, K.A. & Mannix, E.A. (2001). The dynamic nature of conflict: A longitudinal study of intragroup conflict and group performance. *Academy of Management Journal*, 44, 238–251.

Johnson, G., Melin, L. & Whittington, R. (2003). Micro strategy and strategizing: Towards an activity-based view. *Journal of Management Studies*, 40(1), 3–22.

Kotter, J.P. (2001). What leaders really do. *Harvard Business Review*, 79, 85–98.

Le Roy, F. & Czakon, W. (2015). Managing coopetition: The missing link between strategy and performance. *Industrial Marketing Management*, 53, 3–6.

Le Roy, F. & Fernandez, A.S. (2015). Managing coopetitive tensions at the working-group level: The rise of the coopetitive project team. *British Journal of Management*, 26(4), 671–688.

Luo, X., Slotegraaf, R.J. & Pan, X. (2006). Cross-functional "coopetition": The simultaneous role of cooperation and competition within firms. *Journal of Marketing*, 70(2), 67–80.

March, J.G. & Simon, H.A. (1958). *Organizations.* New York: Wiley.

Mariani, M. (2009). *Emergent coopetitive and cooperative strategies in inter-organizational relationships: Empirical evidence from Australian and Italian operas*, in Dagnino, G.B & Rocco, E. (eds.) *Coopetition strategy. Theory, experiments and cases.* London: Routledge.

Mariani, M.M. (2016). Coordination in inter-network co-opetitition: Evidence from the tourism sector. *Industrial Marketing Management*, 53, 103–123.

Mierzejewska, W. (2018). Koopetycja w grupach kapitałowych [Coopetition in business groups], *Zeszyty Naukowe Uniwersytetu Ekonomicznego w Katowicach. Studia Ekonomiczne*, 351, 121–130.

Minà, A. & Dagnino, G.B. (2021). *Foundations of coopetition strategy: A framework for competition and cooperation* (1st ed.). Routledge.

Morgeson, F.P., DeRue, D.S. & Karam, E.P. (2010). Leadership in teams: A functional approach to understanding leadership structures and processes. *Journal of Management*, 36, 5–39.

Nalebuff, B.J. & Brandenburger, A.M. (1997). Co-opetition: Competitive and cooperative business strategies for the digital economy. *Strategy & Leadership*, 25(6), 28–33.

Nesse, S. (2018). How to achieve innovation by collaborating with a competitor? A leadership perspective. *Magma*, 5, 61–70.

Öberg, C., Dahlin, P. & Pesämaa, O. (2020). Tension in networks. *Industrial Marketing Management*, 91, 311–322.

Patton, M.Q. (2002). *Qualitative research and evaluation methods* (3rd ed.). Thousand Oaks, CA: Sage Publications.

Putnam, A.L., Sungkhasettee, V.W. & Roediger, H.L. 2016). Optimizing learning in college: Tips from cognitive psychology. *Perspectives on Psychological Science: A Journal of the Association for Psychological Science*, 11(5), 652–660.

Quinton, S. & Wilson, D. (2016). Tensions and ties in social media networks: Towards a model of understanding business relationship development and business performance enhancement through the use of LinkedIn. *Industrial Marketing Management*, 54, 15–24.

Raza-Ullah, T. (2017). *A theory of experienced paradoxical tension in co-opetitive alliances*. PhD Thesis.

Raza-Ullah, T. (2020). Experiencing the paradox of coopetition: A moderated mediation framework explaining the paradoxical tension–performance relationship. *Long Range Planning*, 53, 101863.

Raza-Ullah, T., Bengtsson, M. & Kock, S. (2014). The coopetition paradox and tension in coopetition at multiple levels. *Industrial Marketing Management*, 43(2), 189–198.

Raza-Ullah, T., Bengtsson, M. & Vanyushyn, V. (2018). *Coopetition capability: What is it?* Routledge Companion to Coopetition Strategies, 1, 1, 219–226.

Ritala, P. (2012). Coopetition strategy – When is it successful? Empirical evidence on innovation and market performance. *British Journal of Management*, 23(3), 307–324.

Ritala, P. & Tidström, A. (2014). Untangling the value-creation and value-appropriation elements of coopetition strategy: A longitudinal analysis on the firm and relational levels. *Scandinavian Journal of Management*, 30(4), 498–515.

Robert, L.P., Denis, A.R. & Hung, Y-T.C. (2009). Individual swift trust and knowledge-based trust in face-to-face and virtual team members. *Journal of Management Information Systems*, 26(2), 241–279.

Schad, J., Lewis, M., Raisch, S. & Smith, W. (2016). Paradox research in management science: Looking back to move forward. *Academy of Management Annals*, 10(1), 5–64.

Schutte, N.S., Manes, R.R. & Malouff, J.M. (2009). Antecedent-focused emotion regulation, response modulation and well-being. *Current Psychology: A Journal for Diverse Perspectives on Diverse Psychological Issues*, 28(1), 21–31.

Seepana, C., Paulraj, A. & Huq, F.A. (2020). The architecture of coopetition: Strategic intent, ambidextrous managers, and knowledge sharing. *Industrial Marketing Management*, 91, 100–113.

Smith, W.K. & Lewis, M.W. (2011). Toward a theory of paradox: A dynamic equilibrium model of organizing. *The Academy of Management Review*, 36(2), 381–403.

Smith, W.K. & Tushman, M.L. (2005). Managing strategic contradictions: A top management model for managing innovation streams. *Organization Science*, 16(5), 522–536.

Staniec, I. & Zakrzewska-Bielawska, A. (2020). *Contemporary challenges in cooperation and coopetition in the age of industry 4.0*. Springer Proceedings in Business and Economics.

Thomas, K.W. & Kilmann, R.H. (1974). *Thomas-Kilmann conflict mode instrument*. Xicom, a subsidiary of CPP Inc, Mountain View, CA.

Tidström, A. (2014). Managing tensions in coopetition. *Industrial Marketing Management*, 43(2), 261–271.

Tidstrom, A. & Rajala, A. (2016). Coopetition strategy as interrelated praxis and practices on multiple levels. *Industrial Marketing Management*, 58, 35–44.

Tsai, W. (2002). Social structure of "coopetition" within a multiunit organization: Coordination, competition, and intraorganizational knowledge sharing. *Organization Science*, 13(2), 179–190.

Tushman, M.L. & O'Reilly, C.A. (1996). Ambidextrous organizations: Managing evolutionary and revolutionary change. *California Management Review*, 38, 8–29.

Vanyushyn, V., Bengtsson, M., Harryson Näsholm, M. & Boter, H. (2017). International coopetition: are the benefits worth the challenges? *GIKA 2017: The 7th Global Innovation and Knowledge Academy Conference*, Lisbon, Portugal, June 28–30, 2017.

Vuori, T. & Huy, Q.N. (2020). Regulating top managers' emotions during strategy making: Nokia's socially distributed approach enabling radical change from mobile phones to networks in 2007–2013. *Academy of Management Journal*, 65(1), 331–361.

Yan, Y., Dong, J.Q. & Faems, D. (2020). Not every coopetitor is the same: The impact of technological, market and geographical overlap with coopetitors on firms' breakthrough inventions. *Long Range Planning*, 53(1), 101873.

4 Coopetition Drivers within Business Groups

Wioletta Mierzejewska and Rumiana Górska

Introduction

Coopetition within business groups is classified as intra-organisational coopetition and can be induced and incentivised by the parent company as well as emergent in nature (Luo, 2005; Song et al., 2016; Mierzejewska, 2018; Lagerström et al., 2021). There are a variety of factors that determine the emergence of coopetition relationships within business groups. Coopetition drivers can be found primarily inside a business group, but they may be also found outside. Coopetition drivers within business groups are partly the same factors determining coopetition between legally and organisationally independent firms, but there is also a wide range of factors specific to business groups and related to their organisation. In the management literature, the need for research on drivers of intra-organisational coopetition is underlined (Ghobadi & D'Ambra, 2012), but only a few studies examine motives/drivers/antecedents of coopetition within complex organisations (Chambers, 2015; Dorn et al., 2016).

The aim of this chapter is to investigate drivers of coopetition within business groups and find the main internal and external coopetition determinants therein. The comprehensive analysis of both external and internal drivers of coopetition within business groups is implemented. This is a new perspective as previous studies mainly examined single driver of intra-organisational coopetition (Tsai, 2002; Song et al., 2016; Strese et al., 2016; Bengid et al., 2018; Knein et al., 2020).

Theoretical Lenses

Despite the development of research on coopetition, drivers of this relationship have been still insufficiently recognised (Czakon et al., 2020). Coopetition drivers include a wide range of factors influencing managers' decisions about engaging in cooperation with competitors. At the inter-organisational level, coopetition drivers are divided into industry-specific and contextual (Bengtsson & Raza-Ullah, 2016; Czakon et al., 2020). The first group of antecedence relates to industry characteristics, technological demands, industry life-cycle phase, existence of regulatory bodies, degree

DOI: 10.4324/9781003324775-5

of change, influential stakeholders, and so on. Contextual antecedents refer to both relationship and internal contexts. The relationship context includes partner and relationship characteristics, while the internal one includes internal goals, capabilities, managerial mindset, experience, and so on (Czakon et al., 2014; Bengtsson & Raza-Ullah, 2016; Dorn et al., 2016). A similar approach, dividing coopetition divers into two groups, can be implemented at the intra-organisational level. However, the set of drivers differs from those identified at inter-organisational level as coopetition characteristic differs (Bengtsson & Raza-Ullah, 2016). The first group of intra-organisational coopetition drivers is related to economy and industry specificity and is similar inter-organisational coopetition drivers. The study refers to them as external ones. The second group of drivers refers to a business group specificity and the study refers to them as internal drivers. Due to fragmentary research on drivers of coopetition within a business group, theoretical framework is based on the analysis of drivers of intra-organisational coopetition (including cross-functional and within multinational corporations).

External Perspective of Coopetition Drivers

Business groups operate globally in different industries, and therefore industry specifics translate into the intensity and types of intra-group relations. Industry specifics refer to the level of uncertainty (especially technological), number and behaviour of competitors, power of regulatory bodies and other stakeholders, phase of industry life cycle and stage of business cycle, and other factors. The uncertainty of the environment resulting from technological, social, and political changes is a factor that encourages cooperation but also fosters internal competition both for resources and in terms of products (Chambers, 2015).

Technological uncertainty and need for innovation positively influence the emergence of coopetition within business groups. Birkinshaw (2001) notices that in high-tech industries, intrinsic competition is very common in many stages of product development and in many forms. In such environment, the parent company, on top of cooperation, encourages competition in technological solutions and innovative projects/products. For example, it can encourage subsidiaries to compete in developing technology that often leads to charter overlap. According to Birkinshaw and Lingblad (2005), no organisation, even a large one, can reasonably expect to understand all the possible technological trajectories in the industry and the full range of economic, social, or political changes to which it is exposed. It is extremely important at an early stage of the industry life cycle when nobody knows which standard or business model will prevail (Birkinshaw & Lingblad, 2005). Thus, internal coopetition can enable success in the market.

Political and social uncertainty also favours coopetition within business groups. Unstable markets in host countries can promote knowledge exchange and simultaneous resource competition. Subsidiaries cooperate with each other to exchange knowledge about the market or sign agreements that increase their local market power. Simultaneously, subsidiaries compete for capital and reinvestments made by the parent company, or for technological support of the parent company, which is to enable better adaptation to local conditions (Luo, 2005). Chambers (2015) observe that uncertainty reflected by the speed of change in customer needs and preferences is a salient external antecedent of inter-subsidiary coopetition. Additionally, the level of homogeneity of customer preferences is the factor influencing internal coopetition. The variety of customer needs encourages the company to maintain a highly (but closely) diversified product portfolio, and if product groups are in separate units, then these units become natural competitors (Birkinshaw & Lingblad, 2005). Liu et al. (2019) argue that intense competition on internal resources and external markets appears when a network of subsidiaries operating in the same industry and offering similar products is settled in the host country. Establishing several subsidiaries from one business group in one host country or region, but operating in different industries, prevents intense internal competition for customers and external markets.

Previous studies focused mostly on different dimensions of environmental uncertainty as a driver of coopetition within complex organisations. However, the list should be extended to include factors, such as competitive pressure, globalisation, innovation and technology intensity of an industry, and phase of business cycle. Under external competitive pressure, subsidiaries cooperate to outperform competitors, but simultaneous competition may emerge on internal resources, parent company support, and investments. Globalisation also influences internal coopetition. In globalised industries, economies of scale and possibility of product standardisation are of great importance. Cooperation between subsidiaries is, therefore, aimed at winning external competitors, and competition within business groups may arise as the strategic domains of the business units begin to overlap (Birkinshaw & Lingblad, 2005). Innovation and technology challenges, especially in high-tech industries, such as increasing R&D costs, shrinking product life cycle, and technology convergence, are seen as external drivers of coopetition. Innovation pressure and need for technological progresses increase the likelihood of internal coopetition (Dziurski, 2020). Additionally, some researchers found that the phase of a business cycle also matters. Subsidiaries were more willing to compete during the growth phase and cooperate in and after a recession, when resources are limited (Chambers, 2015).

Internal Perspective of Coopetition Drivers

The second group of drivers of coopetition within business groups refers to internal factors. Those drivers are related to features and organisation of a business group, specificity of subsidiaries, as well as the managers' characteristics (Chambers, 2015).

At the level of the whole business group, implemented strategy and organisational design are factors of the great importance. Dellestrand et al. (2020) argue that the corporate strategy and headquarter resource allocation strategy influence competitive and cooperative behaviours of subsidiaries. Pursuing an efficiency-focused strategy with minimal relatedness between subsidiaries favour competitive behaviour, while an effectiveness-focused corporate strategy emphasising synergies and economies of scale mainly encourages cooperation. Additionally, Li et al. (2007) notice that competitive and cooperative relationships of subsidiaries in multinational corporations are significantly influenced by the internationalisation strategy pursued by the corporation, as well as structural features, including the role of the parent company, communication system, and reward system. Globally integrated strategies reduce the level of competition between subsidiaries due to clearly defined areas and scopes of their activities. In contrast, nationally independent strategies (like multinational strategy) contribute to the growth of interdependence and cooperation of subsidiaries, but also to the growth of competition between them due to overlapping markets, orientation toward the same clients, lack of regional resources, and subsidiaries' efficiency assessment. Interestingly, some researchers argue that the dualism of competition and cooperation is most visible in the transnational strategy (Luo, 2005; Chambers, 2015).

An issue closely related to the corporate strategy of a business group is its organisational design. The level of centralisation and formalisation, definition of charters, tasks, and competences of subsidiaries as well as communication and reward system influence the type and intensity of internal relations. Dellestrand et al. (2020) argue that subsidiaries' competitive behaviour can be easily traced within business groups that design an organisational structure with subsidiaries evaluation on a stand-alone basis. Previous studies prove that formalisation positively and centralisation negatively influence internal coopetition (Strese et al., 2016). However, Li et al. (2007) suggest that greater centralisation and control of the relationship between subsidiaries allow for the reduction of competition while at the same time encourage cooperation. In line with this, Cerrato (2006) points out that decentralisation may favour an increase in the intensity of competition between units because managers, over time, choose more attractive market areas. Additionally, when rights and obligations, objectives, and market scope of each subsidiary are not clearly defined, conflicts may arise as a basis for competition (Li et al., 2009).

Cooperation and competition within business groups can be stimulated by a reward system. Luo (2005) argues that the incentive system is the main mechanism that drives domestic managers' motivation to constant competition for corporate resources and market expansion. However, a reward system that is based on assessment of individual subsidiary performance (individually based reward system) promotes internal competition, while a systemic reward system contributes more to cooperation between subsidiaries because the assessment of a subsidiary's performance is based on the verification of its contribution to overall corporation performance (Li et al., 2007).

Modern studies of coopetition are increasingly focusing on behavioural issues of this relationship (Czakon et al., 2020). One of them is organisational culture that can be an important driver of cooperative and competitive behaviours. It is argued that an organisational culture focused on cooperation has a positive impact on the search by subsidiaries potential partners to cooperate within a business group, while at the same time competitive behaviour between them is less frequently observed (Chambers, 2015). Knein et al. (2020) prove that all surveyed types of organisational culture (group, development, hierarchy, and rational cultures) influence intra-organisational coopetition and organisational cultural dimensions directly strengthen cross-functional coopetition.

Subsidiaries within business groups are to some extent autonomous (Dellestrand et al., 2020). Thus, the specificity of a subsidiary and its managers is also an important driver of cooperative and competitive behaviours. Subsidiary-specific factors include endowment with resources, location and size, previous relationships, orientation towards entrepreneurship, similarity of offered products, or strategic interdependence (Luo, 2005; Li et al., 2009; Chambers, 2015; Strese et al., 2016; Phookan, 2020). However, the most important driver of intra-organisational coopetition is related to subsidiary resource endowment. Previous studies prove that cooperation is more often established with subsidiaries with rare but useful resources. Such units are perceived as attractive cooperation partners within a business group (Chambers, 2015). Small units strive to cooperate with large and better equipped ones (Tsai, 2002). Competition within a business group is related to similar resource base of subsidiaries. It turns out that the similarity of resources necessary to achieve goals favours competitive behaviour within a business group (Li et al., 2009). Internal competition for resources can also be triggered by capabilities retrogression and loss of a competitive advantage on the market. This could be the consequence of unsuccessful modernisation of resources but also environmental changes. In this situation, foreign units often increase competition among themselves for the parent company resources and corporate support, although at the same time some of them may start working together to strengthen their resources and skills (Luo, 2005). Therefore, the main resource drivers for establishing coopetitive relations are the scarcity of resources, various resource profiles, or pursuit of a more efficient use of resources. It should be noted that unequal resource redistribution forces cooperation both vertically and horizontally but at the same time implies competition for access to resources that are at the disposal of the parent company. Additionally, the struggle for internal resources is more intensive than for resources from the external market (Luo, 2005; Maurer, 2011).

The last group of internal drivers of coopetition within business groups relates to the individual characteristics of managers. Their mindsets, attitudes, and experiences can lead to more cooperative or competitive behaviours. Individual features of managers indicate a greater or lesser willingness to take risks, aggressive management moves, or cooperation. The "winner-take-all" mentality of managers favours intensive inter-organisational competition (Dellestrand et al., 2020). The ambitions of managers are also important as they translate into strategic decisions regarding the position and strategy of the managed unit. Managers of subsidiaries often constantly strive to improve their bargaining power and manifest competitive behaviour towards others but at the same time establish cooperation relations and enter various types of internal coalitions (Phookan, 2020). Some managers show overwhelmingly positive attitudes towards competition as it is inherent in both business interactions and human nature. Others tend to avoid competition and establish cooperative relationships with other entities in a business group (Chambers, 2015).

Empirical Findings

The study, which results are presented in the chapter, uses a survey database of 121 business groups in Poland. It was drawn from the databases of business groups that a parent company is listed on the Warsaw Stock Exchange. Data were acquired from surveys with top managers of parent companies from randomly selected business groups, Amadeus database and financial statements published by business groups. Information about the research sample and method is presented in the introduction. In the study, authors created a scale of new items to identify the most important internal and external drivers of coopetition within business groups, and 18 items were identified. Items from 1 to 8 are classified as external drivers and from 9 to 18 as internal ones. All items were evaluated on a five-point Likert scale (1 – very low impact, 5 – very high impact, with the additional rate 0 meaning no impact) in respect of their impact on the simultaneous competition and cooperation between entities within a business group. The study has applied the factor analysis. This is a statistical technique that describes variability among observed, correlated variables in terms of a potentially lower number of unobserved variables called factors.

Two tests that indicate the suitability of the data for the structure detection were performed. The Bartlett's test of sphericity tests the hypothesis that correlation matrix is an identity matrix, which indicates that variables are unrelated and, therefore, unsuitable for the structure detection. The small value of the significance level indicates that the factor analysis is useful. The Kaiser-Meyer-Olkin (KMO) measure of sampling adequacy is a statistic that indicates the proportion of variance in variables that might be caused by underlying factors. Values close to 1.0 indicate that the factor analysis is useful. If the value is less than 0.5, the results of the factor analysis are not very useful. In the study, those statistics point to satisfactory performance.

The factor analysis is an appropriate and commonly used method when dealing with a large amount of data to facilitate their interpretation. The exploratory factor analysis (EFA) is appropriate for the study as it investigates the structure of data. However, data is of ordinal type (a statistical data type where variables have natural, ordered categories and distances between categories are not known); therefore, the standard use of the explanatory factor analysis causes biased estimates. Lorenzo-Seva and Ferrando (2006) address this problem and developed free software called FACTOR, which was later updated (Ferrando & Lorenzo-Seva, 2017). The latest version of this software (FACTOR 10.10.03) was used in the study. This software is designed to carry out factor analysis for ordered variables.

Different factor models were tested, and multiple approaches available in the FACTOR software for the best outcome were tried. Two methods were used for the factor extraction: robust unweighted least squared method (ULS) and principal component analysis (PCA). Next, the study examined the number of rotations: Varimax, Quartimax, and Equimax. The purpose of the rotation is to obtain more clearly differentiated factor loadings, which is necessary to facilitate interpretation. All these methodical steps allow to identify the main external and internal factors determining simultaneous cooperation and competition in business groups.

External Coopetition Drivers within Business Groups in Poland

In the study, the following external drivers were identified: (1) level of development of the technological environment, (2) customer preferences, (3) industry innovation, (4) industry internationalisation, (5) industry maturity, (6) globalisation, (7) intensity of competition in the industry, and (8) access to capital. Table 4.1 presents descriptive statistics for external drivers of coopetition within a business group based on the study carried.

According to descriptive statistics included in Table 4.1, variables with the greatest mean value are as follow: level of development of the technological environment, intensity of competition in the industry, and customer preferences. Those are drivers rated the highest by respondents. Those variables have leptokurtic distribution (Kurtosis>0), which means that most of answers are relatively close to the average value. The rest of drivers have platykurtic distribution, so the dispersion of answers is higher. All variables have negative-skewed distribution, which means that mode is greater than the mean. The biggest asymmetry is observed for an industry internationalisation, which means that the mass of the distribution is concentrated on the right, so this determinant also seems to have an important impact.

Table 4.1 Descriptive statistics for external drivers of coopetition within a business group

	Category	*Mean*	*Standard deviation*	*Asymmetry*	*Kurtosis*	*Mode*
1	Level of development of the technological environment	3.066	1.34	-1.180	0.350	4
2	Customer preferences	2.744	1.31	-0.992	0.253	3
3	Industry innovation	2.281	1.52	-0.256	-1.017	3
4	Industry internationalisation	2.388	1.66	-0.581	-1.386	4
5	Industry maturity	2.050	1.37	-0.404	-1.143	3
6	Globalisation	2.339	1.39	-0.270	-0.633	3
7	Intensity of competition in the industry	2.992	1.44	-0.806	0.047	3
8	Access to capital	2.686	1.60	-0.390	-0.680	3

Source: Own elaboration.

Table 4.2 Proportion of variance of external drivers explained by common factors

Factors	*Eigenvalue*	*Proportion of variance*	*Cumulative proportion of variance*
F1	2.59	**0.32**	0.32
F2	1.39	**0.18**	0.50
F3	1.00	**0.12**	0.62
F4	0.86	**0.11**	0.73

Source: Own elaboration.

In the study, the factor analysis on the external drivers of intra-organisational coopetition to identify the most important among them was conducted. Two tests that indicate the suitability of the data for the structure detection were performed. The value of the KMO test is 0.70, and the value of the Bartlett's statistic is 171.2 ($p = 0.000010$), so they suggest that the data may be grouped into a smaller set of underlying factors.

Table 4.2 illustrates results of the factor analysis and presents the proportion of variance of analysed variables explained by four common factors.[1] The first common factor accounts for 32% of the variance, the second for 18%, the third for 12%, and the fourth one for 11%.

For better interpretation of factors, the number of rotations were examined. The normalised Varimax rotation provides the most clearly differentiated factor loadings. Results of the factor analysis after rotation of the external drivers of intra-organisational coopetition within a business group are shown in Table 4.3.

The four common factors explain about 73% of the variance. The first factor (F1) accounts for 26% of variance of variables analysed and is most closely related to industry innovation and internationalisation. The second

Table 4.3 Rotated loading matrix for common factor analysis of external drivers

	Variable/Factor	*F1*	*F2*	*F3*	*F4*
	Proportion of variance	*0.26*	*0.19*	*0.17*	*0.11*
1	Level of development of the technological environment		**0.605**		
2	Customer preferences		0.354		
3	Industry innovation	**0.878**			
4	Industry internationalisation	**0.713**			
5	Industry maturity				**0.615**
6	Globalisation			**0.961**	
7	Intensity of competition in the industry		0.486		0.340
8	Access to capital	0.335	0.493		

Source: Own elaboration.
Note: Loadings lower than 0.3 in absolute values are omitted, loadings above 0.5 are bold.

factor (F2) that explains 19% of the variance is related to level of development of the technological environment, while the third factor (F3) explaining 17% of variance is related to globalisation. The last common factor (F4) refers mostly to industry maturity and accounts for 11% of the variance. Thus, the common factor analysis reveals that among external drivers the most important ones are as follow: globalisation, level of development of the technological environment, industry innovation with industry internationalisation, and industry maturity. All those drivers are symptoms of environment uncertainty. It can, therefore, be assumed that the environment uncertainty is a crucial determinant among external drivers of coopetition within a business group. According to the literature review, environment uncertainty is shown by the great speed and magnitude of changes (Birkinshaw & Lingblad, 2005). Those changes are often caused by technology, globalisation, and innovation development (Birkinshaw & Lingblad, 2005; Ritala et al., 2009; Bouncken & Kraus, 2013; Dziurski, 2020). Thus, the study supports the view that technological, social, and political uncertainty encourages cooperation and simultaneously fosters competition within a business group (Chambers, 2015).

Internal Coopetition Drivers within Business Groups in Poland

The study focuses on internal drivers related to business group's organisation and strategy as well as subsidiary specificity. It does not consider the perspective of individual managers as the study deals with the perspective of the whole business group. Internal coopetition drivers include following drivers: (9) internationalisation of the business group, (10) business group age, (11) business group size, (12) implemented strategy, (13) structure of

Table 4.4 Descriptive statistics for internal drivers of coopetition with a business group

	Category	*Mean*	*Standard deviation*	*Asymmetry*	*Kurtosis*	*Mode*
9	Internationalisation of business groups	1.975	1.51	−0.396	−1.576	3
10	Business group age	1.702	1.26	−0.302	−1.554	3
11	Business group size	2.496	1.21	−0.969	0.003	3
12	Implemented strategy	2.835	1.46	−0.793	−0.313	4
13	Business group structure	2.554	1.47	−0.640	−0.546	3
14	Interdependence of units	2.777	1.43	−0.938	−0.108	3
15	Complexity of business groups	2.455	1.27	−0.831	−0.336	3
16	Resource endowment of units	2.471	1.37	−0.722	−0.674	3
17	Centralisation of activities	2.587	1.39	−0.853	−0.602	3
18	Characteristics of shareholders	2.240	1.48	−0.158	−1.034	3

Source: Own elaboration.

the business group, (14) interdependence of units, (15) complexity of the business group, (16) resource endowment of units, (17) centralisation of activities, and (18) characteristics of shareholders. Table 4.4 presents descriptive statistics for internal drivers of coopetition within business groups based on the study carried.

According to the descriptive statistics presented in Table 4.4, variables with the greatest mean value are as follow: implemented strategy, interdependence of units, and centralisation of activities. Distribution of all variables (except business group size) is platykurtic (Kurtosis <0), so the dispersion of the answers is relatively high. Similarly, to external drivers, the distributions of internal ones are also negatively skewed. The biggest asymmetry is observed for business group size, so this determinant may also be significant.

To identify internal drivers of coopetition, another factor analysis was conducted following the same procedure as indicated above. Table 4.5 illustrates results of the factor analysis and presents the proportion of variance of variables analysed that is explained by four common factors. The first common factor accounts for 33% of the variance, the second for 14%, the third for 11%, and the fourth one for 10%. The value of the KMO test is 0.70, and the value of the Bartlett's statistic is 301.0 ($p = 0.00010$), so the internal drivers may also be grouped into a smaller set of underlying factors.

The number of rotations was investigated in the next stage of the research project, and the best interpretation of factors enables normalised Varimax rotation. Results of the factor analysis of internal drivers of coopetition within a business group are shown in Table 4.6.

The four common factors explain about 68% of the variance. The first factor (F1) accounts for 22% of the variance of variables analysed and is most closely related to business group size and level of resource endowment

Table 4.5 Proportion of variance of internal drivers explained by common factors

Factors	*Eigenvalue*	*Proportion of variance*	*Cumulative proportion of variance*
F1	3.35	**0.33**	0.33
F2	1.38	**0.14**	0.47
F3	1.12	**0.11**	0.58
F4	0.95	**0.10**	0.68

Source: Own elaboration.

Table 4.6 Rotated loading matrix for common factor analysis of internal drivers

Variable\Factor		*F1*	*F2*	*F3*	*F4*
Proportion of variance		*0.22*	*0.18*	*0.18*	*0.1*
9	Internationalisation of the business group				0.322
10	Business group age			**0.502**	
11	Business group size	**0.970**			
12	Implemented strategy				**0.749**
13	Business group size	0.407			
14	Interdependence of units		**0.750**		
15	Complexity of business groups		**0.569**	0.359	
16	Resource endowment of units	**0.587**			0.350
17	Centralisation of activities		**0.525**	−0.429	0.383
18	Characteristics of shareholders				**0.580**

Source: own elaboration.
Note: Loadings lower than 0.3 in absolute values are omitted, and loadings above 0.5 are bold.

of units. The second factor (F2), explaining 18% of the variance, is related to interdependence of units, complexity of the business group, and centralisation of activities. The third factor (F3), which explains 18% of the variance, is related to business group age. The fourth factor (F4) accounts for 10% of the variance and refers to implemented strategy and shareholder characteristics. The common factor analysis reveals that among internal drivers the most important are following factors: interdependence of units, complexity of the business group, centralisation of activities, business group size and age, implemented strategy, characteristics of shareholder, as well as the level of resource endowment of units. It is expected that corporate strategy and organisational design of the business group are crucial internal drivers, as they are frequently mentioned in the literature (Li et al., 2007; Chambers, 2015). The factor analysis partly supports this view. It is found that implemented strategy and characteristics of shareholder explain

10% of the variance (factor F4), while two other factors (F1 and F3), which can be classified as organisational design, account for 43% of variance. Additionally, age of the business group is found to be an important internal determinant of coopetition within a business group.

Conclusion

Business groups are complex organisations with different relationships linking units therein. A wide variety of factors influencing the coopetition relationship within a business group can, therefore, be observed. There are external drivers related to the environment in which business groups operate and internal drivers related to the specificity of a business group. The internal ones are very diverse and should be considered at various levels. Most of them are related to characteristics of the business group, its strategy, and organisation. However, equally important are drivers related to individual subsidiaries involved in the relationship, such as the level of resource endowment, size of units, their interdependence, and others. The last subgroup of internal drivers is the type of subsidiaries' managers. After all, it is they who make key decisions. Their attitudes, skills, and commitment may affect both the intensity of cooperation and competition with a business group.

In the study, it was investigated which factors dominate among external and internal ones. It turns out that the most important external drivers of coopetition are as follow: globalisation, level of development of the technological environment, industry innovation and internationalisation, and industry maturity. Those drivers of coopetition within a business group could be classified as an environmental uncertainty. Previous studies argue that changes in technological, social, economic, or political sphere of the environment are important contributors to internal coopetition (Chambers, 2015). Findings of the study are in line with this view. Especially globalisation, internationalisation, technological changes, and industry innovation are important drivers enhancing coopetition between subsidiaries within a business group.

The second group of coopetition drivers within a business group focuses on intra-group features. It is found that the most important internal drivers of coopetition within business groups are as follow: interdependence of units, complexity of the business group, centralisation of activities, resource of units, business group size and age, implemented strategy, and characteristics of shareholders. The first four drivers are related to the organisational design of a business group. It is argued that the organisational design as well as corporate strategy are crucial drivers of coopetition within a business group. This is in line with other studies that prove the importance of organisational conditions on intra-organisational coopetition (Schmid & Maurer, 2008; Seran et al., 2016; Strese et al., 2016). Business groups represent a specific organisational model halfway between the market and hierarchy, and they are perceived as a kind of network and platform to share and exchange resources (Chang & Hong, 2002; Hsieh et al., 2010; Popli et al., 2017). Internal solutions, therefore, influence relationships between subsidiaries and can also enhance coopetition. This resource necessity as well as some degree of autonomy given to subsidiaries promote not only cooperative but also competitive behaviour. Simultaneously, the strategy implemented by the parent company and its behaviour towards subsidiaries influence the intensity of coopetition (Luo, 2005; Li et al., 2007; Chambers, 2015; Dellestrand et al., 2020).

To conclude, in large and complex organisations, like business groups, coopetition is driven by environment uncertainty, internal organisation, and strategy implemented by the parent company. The significance of environmental uncertainty is a factor-linking research on coopetition drivers at the intra- and inter-organisational level. However, internal drivers may be of greater importance due to the specificity of a business group. This requires further research, even though the study has given some insight into the matter.

Note

1 The study sets the number of factors extracted using the eigenvalue criterion. To ensure a good validity of the results, loadings above 0.5 were considered. Hair et al. (2010) suggest that the appropriate factor loadings value be dependent on the sample size. As the sample size is 121, the factor loadings should be above 0.5.

References

Bengtsson, M. & Raza-Ullah, T. (2016). A systematic review of research on coopetition: Toward a multilevel understanding. *Industrial Marketing Management*, 57, 23–39.

Birkinshaw, J. (2001). Strategies for managing internal competition. *California Management Review*, 44(1), 21–38.

Birkinshaw, J. & Lingblad, M. (2005). Intrafirm competition and charter evolution in the multibusiness firm. *Organization science*, 16(6), 674–686.

Cerrato, D. (2006). The multinational enterprise as an internal market system. *International Business Review*, 15(3), 253–277.

Chambers, M. (2015). *Dynamic inter-subsidiary relationships of competition and collaboration*. Dissertation. Cranfield University.

Chang, S.J. & Hong, J. (2002). How much does the business group matter in Korea? *Strategic Management Journal*, 23(3), 265–274.

Czakon, W., Mucha-Kuś, K. & Rogalski, M. (2014). Coopetition research landscape: A systematic literature review 1997–2010. *Journal of Economics & Management*, 17, 122–150.

Czakon, W., Klimas, P. & Mariani, M. (2020). Behavioral antecedents of coopetition: A synthesis and measurement scale. *Long Range Planning*, 53(1), 101875.

Dellestrand, H., Kappen, P. & Lindahl, O. (2020). Headquarter resource allocation strategies and subsidiary competitive or cooperative behavior: Achieving a fit for value creation. *Journal of Organization Design*, 9(1), 1–16.

Dorn, S., Schweiger, B. & Albers, S. (2016). Levels, phases and themes of coopetition: A systematic literature review and research agenda. *European Management Journal*, 34(5), 484–500.

Dziurski, P. (2020). Interplay between coopetition and innovation: Systematic literature review. *Organization and Management*, 1(188), 9–20.

Ghobadi, S. & D'Ambra, J. (2012). Coopetitive relationships in cross-functional software development teams: How to model and measure? *Journal of Systems and Software*, 85(5), 1096–1104.

Hsieh, T.J., Yeh, R.S. & Chen, Y.J. (2010). Business group characteristics and affiliated firm innovation: The case of Taiwan. *Industrial Marketing Management*, 39(4), 560–570.

Knein, E., Greven, A., Bendig, D. & Brettel, M. (2020). Culture and cross-functional coopetition: The interplay of organizational and national culture. *Journal of International Management*, 26(2), 100731.

Lagerström, K., Leite, E. & Pahlberg, C. (2021). *Cooperating while competing in multinational corporations*, in Arora-Jonsson, S., Brunsson, N., Hasse, R. & Lagerström, K. (eds.) *Competition: What it is and why it happens*. New York: Oxford University Press.

Li, D., Ferreira, M.P. & Serra, F.R. (2007). *Technology transfer within MNEs: An investigation of inter-subsidiary competition and cooperation*. ADVANTAGE Working Paper, No.1, Instituto Politécnicode Leiria, Leiria.

Li, D., Ferreira, M.P. & Serra, F.R. (2009). Technology transfer within MNEs: Inter-subsidiary competition and cooperation. *RAI-Revista de Administração e Inovação*, 6(1), 139–158.

Liu, Y., Jiao, J. & Xia, J. (2019). Subsidiary networks and foreign subsidiary performance: A coopetition perspective. *Management and Organization Review*, 15(1), 111–143.

Luo, Y. (2005). Toward coopetition within a multinational enterprise: A perspective from foreign subsidiaries. *Journal of World Business*, 40(1), 71–90.

Maurer, J. (2011). *Relationships between foreign subsidiaries: Competition and cooperation in multinational plant engineering companies*. Wiesbaden: Springer Science & Business Media.

Mierzejewska, W. (2018). Koopetycja w grupach kapitałowych [Coopetition in business groups]. *Studia Ekonomiczne*, 351, 121–130.

Phookan H (2020) *Interpersonal cross border knowledge transfer within the multinational enterprise: Subsidiary power, intra-MNE competition and cultural intelligence*. Unpublished doctoral dissertation, Victoria University of Wellington.

Popli, M., Ladkani, R.M. & Gaur, A.S. (2017). Business group affiliation and post-acquisition performance: An extended resource-based view. *Journal of Business Research*, 81, 21–30.

Schmid, S. & Maurer, J. (2008). *Relationships between MNC subsidiaries – towards a classification scheme*. Working paper, 35, ESCP-EAP European School of Management, Berlin.

Seran, T., Pellegrin-Boucher, E. & Gurau, C. (2016). The management of coopetitive tensions within multi-unit organizations. *Industrial Marketing Management*, 53, 31–41.

Song, J., Lee, K. & Khanna, T. (2016). Dynamic capabilities at Samsung: Optimizing internal co-opetition. *California Management Review*, 58(4), 118–140.

Strese, S., Meuer, M.W., Flatten, T.C. & Brettel, M. (2016). Organizational antecedents of cross-functional coopetition: The impact of leadership and organizational structure on cross-functional coopetition. *Industrial Marketing Management*, 53, 42–55.

Tsai, W. (2002). Social structure of "coopetition" within a multiunit organization: Coordination, competition, and intraorganizational knowledge sharing. *Organization Science*, 13(2), 179–190.

5 Coopetition and Subsidiaries' Resource Endowment

Mateusz Juchniewicz

Introduction

The availability and access to suitable resources are one of the core efficiency drivers of organisations. Resources should be appropriate to nature, volume, and complexity of tasks assigned to organisations' members. This means that managers should strive to secure as many high-quality resources as possible. Simultaneously, organisations compete with others for a limited pool of resources. Both phenomena can be observed not only between standalone firms but, more importantly, also in intra-organisational coopetition within a business group. On the one hand, subsidiaries can cooperate to secure and maintain valuable resources to achieve set goals, but, on the other hand, it is also possible for them to compete for resources within a business group that lead to heightened competition. Thus, this chapter aims to elaborate the relationship between subsidiaries' resources endowment and coopetition within a business group considering different types of coopetition based on the intensity of cooperation and competition as well as direction of coopetition.

Theoretical Lenses

A resource can be defined in many ways depending on the adopted perspective. In economics and management, a resource can be defined as "a valuable, useful thing or possession that is being used by an organisation in order to achieve its goals" (Pszczołowski, 1978: 292–293) or as "a natural, human, or manufactured item that helps produce goods and services; a productive agent or factor of production" (McConnell et al., 2011: G-24).

Resources could be divided into tangible and intangible ones. Kerzner (2005) shows that human (knowledge, skills, capacities, talents), physical (real estate, equipment, distribution networks, capacity for sustained deliveries, land), organisational (organisational structure, management offices, planning, monitoring and control systems, policies, and procedures), and financial resources (cash, creditworthiness, credit lines, relationships with banks) are regarded as tangible resources, while organisational culture, reputation, brand name, patents, trademarks, know-how, relationships

DOI: 10.4324/9781003324775-6

with customers, as well as suppliers and social responsibility (special type of an intangible resource showing the public expectation that a firm will make decisions suiting the best the interest of the public) are perceived as intangible resources.

Tangibility characteristic of a resource is a basic one; however, the literature also provides different approaches. Utility defines the ability of a resource to create value for clients, organisations, and environment. Resource utility may be understood differently by different organisations, e.g. raw materials are value creators for production firms; data and information are value creators for ICT firms and human capital for consulting businesses. Rarity and ease of obtaining of a resource are important characteristics too. Rarity is a strong factor creating value of a resource. Rarity of a resources may be linked to high demand for such resource or social agreement that such resource is perceived as valuable (e.g. gold). Ease of obtaining does not have to relate to rarity, but rather to possible technical difficulties in acquisition of a resource. Ease of imitation or substitution means that if any resource is easily replaceable or it can be copied by competitors or partners, it is not recognised as valuable for a firm. Therefore, many firms invest in R&D projects, which are aimed to develop new technologies enabling them to eliminate the advantage of competitors that hold difficult to substitute resources. Durability means that some resources can last for many years without losing value, but less durable resources need to be replaced on a regular basis. Transferability is another characteristic that relates to ability to transfer resources between different entities and low transferability of a resource leads to a more cautious purchase or investment due to high costs.

If two core drivers of coopetition are a competitive pressure, on the one hand, and a desire for cooperation, on the other hand, (Zakrzewska-Bielawska, 2013), controlling resources, having potential access to them and their characteristics, such as utility, rarity, and transferability, constitute one of the main determinants of the scope and scale of coopetition. It is also true for coopetition in a business group, in which the allocation of resources to subsidiaries is important. The resource-based theory implies that a subsidiary's position within a business group, its individual strength, and ability to justify its existence depend on the allocation of resources, technology, knowledge, and experience (Penrose, 1959).

Characteristics of resources largely determine their importance to an organisation and, consequently, their impact on coopetition. It can be assumed that resources that are rare, difficult to imitate or substitute, and contribute greatly to the value creation can drive competition and encourage cooperation. Studies show that securing access to resources is one of the main factors encouraging coopetition (Das et al., 2000, Lavie, 2006; Zakrzewska-Bielawska, 2013), and having access to valuable resources is one of the main benefits of coopetition (Cygler et al., 2018). However, not all kinds of resources influence the coopetition equally.

Considering three main characteristics of resources – rarity, ease of imitation, and impact on value creation – the golden mean concept can be suggested. It means the existence of a certain range that increases the propensity of coopetition as it is illustrated on Figure 5.1.

According to the concept of golden mean, three following behaviours can be mainly observed. First, organisation has secured very rare resources, their ease of imitating or substitution is low, they have a decisive impact on value creation, and it does not encourage coopetition. Organisation having access to such resources is instead inclined to remain within the competition sphere, because its resources give it a lasting competitive advantage and thus no reason for coopetition. This is partially confirmed by the research conducted by Zakrzewska-Bielawska (2013), in which only in one of the categories of resources, market (i.e. brand, reputation, customer loyalty, etc.), companies not engaging in coopetition are better equipped than those that are involved in coopetition. For all other categories of resources (material, financial, competence, information, relations with research centres), companies surveyed show a worse level of equipment in the case of not engaging in coopetition. Second, organisation that holds available and imitable resources that do not significantly contribute to the value creation may show interest in cooperation. It allows organisation to acquire more valuable resources and competition with rivals, that are better equipped with more valuable resources, is hindered. Third, organisation has resources of moderate rarity, not easily imitated, or substituted,

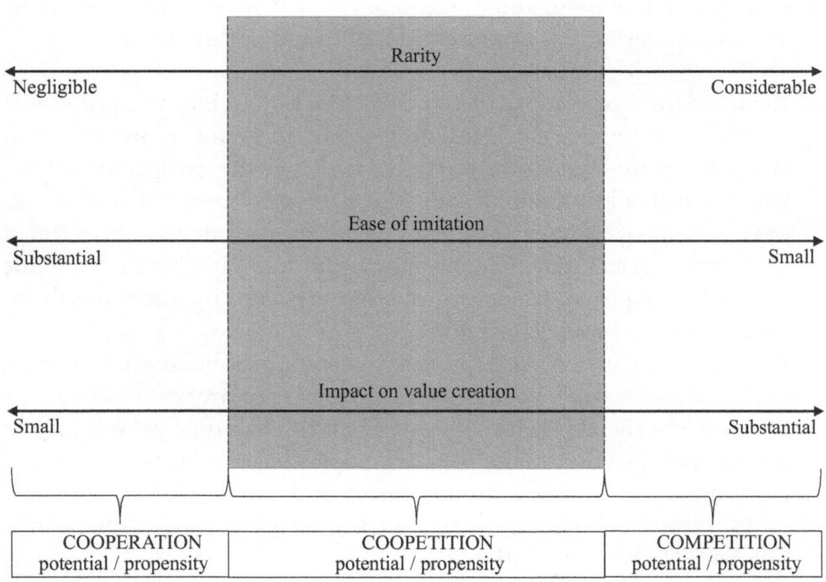

Figure 5.1 Resource' characteristics and the propensity to coopetition.
Source: Own elaboration.

but ones that are viable and have a somewhat significant impact on the value creation (marked grey on the figure). In this scenario, coopetition may be the one strategy that brings the most value to participants.

Coopetition occurs at different levels – individual, intra-organisational, inter-organisational, and network. At individual level, resource coopetition may include, for example, the work of project team members. At intra-organisational level, coopetition takes place, for example, between departments within one organisation and within a business group. Inter-organisational coopetition occurs between different organisations, e.g. within one industry or value chain. Network level coopetition refers to coopetition between networks (or also clusters) (Maripuu, 2018). It should be emphasised, however, that in the case of inter-organisational coopetition, organisations show a willingness to initiate that process, while in the case of intra-organisational coopetition within a business group may be forced by a decision of the parent company. In terms of resources, one can observe the phenomenon of cooperation of subsidiaries on, for example, common project and simultaneously competition for parent firm's resources (Seran et al., 2016).

Coopetition can be found at different levels in an organisation, and on each level, it is possible to observe different propensity to coopetition depending on the characteristics of controlled resources. It must, however, be emphasised that in case of a business group the situation may be different. Subsidiaries are not fully independent in their decisions about partners, structures, and quality of resources. This means that they are not completely free to choose and implement the best strategy for their interests and owned resources. Thus, it can lead to sub optimalisation:

- the need for two companies to compete within a business group in a situation where it is not justified does not allow for improvement of their competitiveness or attractiveness. From the perspective of resources available to subsidiaries, the flow of resources becomes restricted and operational efficiency drops as a result (e.g. investment expenses to get a rarely used machine occur in both subsidiaries, while it may be bought by one entity and be easily used by different subsidiaries within a business group),
- cooperation may become a necessity when one subsidiary in a business group controls unique resources that are particularly difficult to imitate and/or crucial for the value creation. In consequence, resource of a well-equipped subsidiary loses its competitive advantage, and its recreation may be hard or even impossible to do; most of the know-how is transferred without limitation to other subsidiaries (Lavie, 2006; Ghobadi & D'Ambra, 2011).

Controlled resources by subsidiaries may be a driver of either cooperative or competitive behaviours. Cooperative relationships are usually established with companies controlling rare but useful resources. Such companies are perceived as attractive cooperation partners by sister-subsidiaries (Chambers, 2015). Competition among subsidiaries, by contrast, may arise from the similarity of the resource bases needed to meet their respective objectives. It turns out that the greater subsidiaries' demand for similar resources, the more predisposed they are to competitive behaviours (Li et al., 2009). Thus, resource shortages, diverse resource portfolios, and aspirations to more effective utilisation of resources can be identified as the main resource-related drivers for entering coopetitive relationships. It must be noted that uneven availability of resources compels both vertical and horizontal cooperation, but at the same time, it implies competition for access to resources controlled by the parent company. Additionally, the struggle for internal resources is often characterised by more intense rivalry than the competition for resources found outside a business group (Maurer, 2011).

In the discussion on resource endowment and coopetition, it is expedient to make a reference to scale and link alliances. The first one involves contributions that are similar, while the second one refers to situations when partners' resource contribution differs significantly (Mitchell, 2002). In effect, in the case of link alliances, the main goal is a business growth, such as expansion to new markets, and in the scale alliances, the economies of scale and improvement of the efficiency of existing businesses. This taxonomy is like Sakakibara's (1997) proposal that distinguishes cost-sharing and skill-sharing alliances. In this case, firms looking at coopetition seek scale alliances when their resource bases are similar as it is the only way they can avail themselves of the economies of scale. Additionally, their production profiles are similar, and they are desirous to pursue R&D activities. By contrast, a greater propensity to link alliances occurs when firms have different geographic origins and sizes, and they desire for the integration of value chains (e.g. linking resources in distribution with resources in sales).

Empirical Findings

The study, which results are presented in the chapter, uses a survey database of 121 business groups in Poland that was drawn from the databases of business groups that a parent company is listed on the Warsaw Stock Exchange. Data were acquired from surveys with top managers of parent companies from randomly selected business groups, Amadeus database and financial statements published by business groups. Information about the research sample and method is presented in the introduction, while measures of coopetition and coopetition types are elaborated in Chapter 2.

This chapter discusses results of the study on the subsidiaries' resource endowment in the context of coopetition within a business group. In the study, respondents were asked to grade the subsidiaries' resources endowment on a five-point Likert scale, where 1 means very poor and 5 means very good. Table 5.1 presents the basic statistics regarding the question on the subsidiaries' resource endowment.

Table 5.1 shows that none of respondents graded the subsidiaries' resource endowment as very poor or poor. Few respondents indicated to medium subsidiaries' resource endowment (9.9%), and the majority rated it as good (59.5%) and very good (30.6%). One of reasons for such distribution of responses is the research sample. On the one hand, only business groups listed on the Warsaw Stock Exchange are selected; on the other hand, respondents represent parent companies in business groups. Therefore, the results should be interpreted with high caution.

The study aims also to examine the relationship between subsidiaries' resource endowment from the parent company perspective and coopetition. In the study, four- and nine-field matrixes of coopetition are used (see Chapter 2). In the four-field matrix, the intensity of cooperation and competition is divided into low and high, while in the nine-field matrix is split into low, medium, and high. Table 5.2 presents the results of the chi-squared test on relationship between subsidiaries' resource endowment and coopetition types based on four-field coopetition matrix.

In four-field coopetition matrix, only two types of coopetition are identified. First type is coopetition with low cooperation and competition, and the second type is coopetition with high cooperation and low

Table 5.1 Subsidiaries' resources endowment within business groups

Resource endowment	*Frequency*	*Percentage*	*Cumulative percentage*
3 – Medium	12	9.9	9.9
4 – Good	72	59.5	69.4
5 – Very good	37	30.6	100.0
Total	121	100.0	

Source: Own elaboration.

Table 5.2 Coopetition types based on four-field coopetition matrix versus subsidiaries' resource endowment

Coopetition type	*Subsidiaries' resource endowment*		
	Medium	*Good*	*Very good*
Low cooperation and competition	17%	10%	16%
High cooperation and low competition	83%	90%	84%
Total	100% (N = 12)	100% (N = 72)	100% (N = 37)

Source: Own elaboration.
$p = 0.556$; $\chi^2 = 1.173$.

Table 5.3 Coopetition types based on nine-field coopetition matrix versus subsidiaries' resource endowment

Coopetition type	*Subsidiaries' resource endowment*		
	Medium	*Good*	*Very good*
Low cooperation and competition	0%	0%	3%
Medium cooperation and low competition	8%	6%	14%
Medium cooperation and competition	8%	4%	0%
High cooperation and low competition	76%	69%	51%
High cooperation and medium competition	8%	21%	32%
Total	100% (N = 12)	100% (N = 72)	100% (N = 37)

Source: Own elaboration.
$p = 0.225$; $\chi^2 = 10.599$.

competition. The chi-squared test does not confirm the relationship between subsidiaries' resource endowment and coopetition within business groups as it is not statistically significant. It can be stated that, regardless subsidiaries' resource endowment, dominate type is coopetition with high cooperation and low competition. However, business groups with good subsidiaries' resource endowment implement more often coopetition with high cooperation and low competition that business groups with medium and high subsidiaries' resource endowment.

Table 5.3 presents the results of the chi-squared test on relationship between subsidiaries' resource endowment and coopetition types based on nine-field coopetition matrix.

In nine-field coopetition matrix, five types of coopetition (out of nine possible) are identified as it is indicated in Table 5.3. The diversification in the number of observations in different group makes it difficult to achieve statistically significant results. It is confirmed by the chi-squared test that is not statistically significant. Similarly, to the results on coopetition types based on four-field coopetition matrix versus subsidiaries' resource endowment, there is not relationship between intra-group coopetition and subsidiaries' resource endowment. However, some conclusions can be made. First, business groups surveyed aim at coopetition with high cooperation regardless subsidiaries' resource endowment. Second, regardless subsidiaries' resource endowment, business groups prefer low competition over medium one. Third, coopetition with high cooperation and low competition is implemented predominantly by business groups with medium subsidiaries' resource endowment. Fourth, business groups with

Table 5.4 Coopetition types based on its direction versus subsidiaries' resource endowment

Coopetition types	*Subsidiaries' resource endowment*		
	Medium	*Good*	*Very good*
Unidirectional coopetition	17%	10%	0%
Network coopetition	83%	90%	100%
Total	100% (N=12)	100% (N=72)	100% (N=37)

Source: Own elaboration.
$p = 0.082$; $\chi^2 = 5.003$.

good and very good subsidiaries' resource endowment tend to implement coopetition with high cooperation and medium competition more often than those with medium subsidiaries' resource endowment.

The next step in the research process was to test the relationship between subsidiaries' resource endowment and coopetition types considering its direction. Two main coopetition types are identified: unidirectional and network. The results of the chi-squared test are presented in Table 5.4.

Unidirectional coopetition refers to simultaneous cooperation and competition in one direction: vertical or horizontal, while network coopetition refers to simultaneous cooperation and competition in multiple directions within a business group (see Chapter 2). Results exhibit some correlation between subsidiaries' resource endowment and type of coopetition. What is interesting, none of business groups surveyed with very good subsidiaries' resource endowment pursue unidirectional coopetition. The chi-squared test confirms partially differences in subsidiaries' resource endowment in business groups that implement unidirectional and network coopetition as the asymptotic significance reached 0.082. This means that results are statistically significant as confidence level is set as 90%. But, it is still weak evidence on the relationship between subsidiaries' resource endowment and coopetition types based on its direction.

The results of the study do not allow formulate strong and unambiguous conclusion on the relationship between coopetition subsidiaries' resource endowment. However, they confirm to some extend results of previous studies presented in the literature. It can be concluded that gaining access to resources beyond the subsidiary's reach can be the main factor driving coopetition. In general, business groups surveyed, regardless subsidiaries' resource endowment, are focused on coopetition with high level of cooperation and avoid one with medium or high level of competition.

Conclusion

The literature and business practice show that resource endowment is an important determinant of coopetition, and it can impact its intensity, direction, and domination either of cooperation or competition. Previous studies focus mainly on standalone firms, and the assumption on the relationship between resource endowment and coopetition may be distorted if coopetition within a business group is examined. This is because different, mainly political, factors may affect coopetition within a business group. Unfortunately, results of the empirical study do not confirm that there is relationship between subsidiaries' resource endowment and coopetition identified based on the intensity of cooperation and competition. It is only found that there exists a weak correlation between subsidiaries' resource endowment and coopetition types identified based on the direction of coopetition. In all other cases, no statistically significant correlation is identified. However, the topic of subsidiaries' resource endowment and coopetition is an interesting field for further, more in-depth studies that could include the impact of the type of a resource on the intensity of coopetition, assessment of resources' endowment from perspective of different entities within a business group, and importance of resource endowment in the coopetition decision-making process on the level of the parent company.

References

Chambers, M. (2015). *Dynamic, inter-subsidiary relationships of competition and collaboration.* Doctoral Dissertation, Cranfield University.

Chen, S.-J., Lawler, J.J. & Bae, J. (2005). Convergence in human resource systems: A comparison of locally owned and MNC subsidiaries in Taiwan. *Human Resource Management*, 44, 237–256.

Cygler, J., Sroka, W., Solesvik, M. & Dębkowska K. (2018). Benefits and drawbacks of coopetition: The roles of scope and durability in coopetitive relationships. *Sustainability*, 10(8), 1–24.

Dagnino, G.B. & Padula, G. (2002). *Coopetition strategy: A new kind of interfirm dynamics for value creation.* Paper presented at 2nd EURAM Annual Conference, Stockholm 2002, May 9–11.

Das, T.K. & Teng, B.S. (200). A resource-based theory of strategic alliances. *Journal of Management*, 26(1), 31–61.

de Wit, B. & Meyer, R. (1998). *Strategy: Process, content, context. An international perspective.* London: International Thomson Business Press.

Ghobadi, S. & D'Ambra, J. (2011). Coopetitive knowledge sharing: An analytical review of literature. *The Electronic Journal of Knowledge Management*, 9(4), 307–317.

Kerzner, H. (2005). *Advanced project management.* Hoboken, NJ: John Wiley and Sons.

Lavie, D. (2006). The competitive advantage of interconnected firms: An extension of the resource-based view. *Academy of Management Review*, 31(3), 638–658.

Li, D., Ferreira, M.P. & Serra F.R. (2009). Technology transfer within MNEs: Inter-subsidiary competition and cooperation. *RAI-Revista de Administração e Inovação*, 6(1), 139–158.

Luo, Y. (2005). Toward coopetition within a multinational enterprise: A perspective from foreign subsidiaries. *Journal of World Business*, 40(1), 71–90.

Maripuu, V. (2018). E-invoice service providers interoperability: Coopetitive strategy in Europe. Master Thesis, Tartu, https://dspace.ut.ee/bitstream/handle/10062/61187/maripuu_vivian.pdf?sequence=1&isAllowed=y (Accessed: 9 June 2022).

Maurer, J. (2011). *Relationships between foreign subsidiaries: Competition and cooperation in multinational plant engineering companies*. Wiesbaden: Springer Science & Business Media.

McConnell, C.R., Brue, S.L. & Flynn, S.M. (2011). *Economics: Principles, problems, and policies* (19th ed.). New York: McGraw-Hill/Irwin.

Mitchell, W., Dussauge, P. & Garrette, B. (2002). Alliances with competitors: How to combine and protect key resources? *Creativity and Innovation Management*, 11(3), 203–223.

Penrose, E.T. (1959). *The theory of the growth of the firm*. New York: Wiley.

Pszczołowski, T. (1978). Mała encyklopedia prakseologii i teorii organizacji [Little encyclopedia of praxeology and theory of organization]. Wrocław, Warszawa, Kraków, Gdańsk: Zakład Narodowy Imienia Ossolińskich.

Sakakibara, M. (1997). Heterogeneity of firm capabilities and cooperative research and development: An empirical examination of motives. *Strategic Management Journal*, 18, 143–164.

Seran, T., Pellegrin-Boucher, E. & Gurau, C. (2016). The management of coopetitive tensions within multi-unit organizations. *Industrial Marketing Management*, 53, 31–41.

Zakrzewska-Bielawska, A. (2013). Coopetition as a factor in the development of innovative and technologically advanced firms: an example of the high-tech sector. *Proceedings of the International Symposium on Business and Management*. Knowledge Association of Taiwan, Kitakyushu.

6 Coopetition within International Business Groups

Mirosław Jarosiński

Introduction

Business groups fall within the area of interest of international business (Dau et al., 2021), but so far, they have received much less attention than they should have (Aguilera et al., 2020). It is crucial to understand business groups (Holmes et al., 2018), but "little attention has been paid to the internationalisation of business groups" (Aguilera et al., 2020: 2), and in the case of business groups, internationalisation is considered an important strategic decision, especially if they originate from emerging markets (Shukla & Akbar, 2018). Therefore, understanding what lies at the heart of business groups' internationalisation is extremely important for their functioning (Kumar et al., 2012).

Although there are many definitions of internationalisation, in this chapter, internationalisation is understood as "the process by which an enterprise establishes relationships with other entities in order to sell or purchase products on foreign markets, or for other purposes related to improving its international competitiveness, achieving as a result of this process a certain state (level) of internationalisation" (Jarosiński, 2013: 19).

The aim of this chapter is to show the relationship between coopetition within business groups and their internationalisation.

The chapter is organised as follows. First, a brief literature review regarding internationalisation of business groups is presented. Second, the relation between coopetition of business group's subsidiaries and the group's internationalisation is elaborated. Third, the study method and study results are introduced. Fourth, conclusion is developed, followed by limitations of the study and suggestions for future research directions.

Theoretical Lenses

According to Dau et al. (2021), business groups or firms belonging to them position themselves better on international markets than independent enterprises undertaking internationalisation due to greater and easier

DOI: 10.4324/9781003324775-7

access to resources (including capital). Also, Carney et al. (2017) observe that business groups may create opportunities for their affiliates to obtain capital and other resources internally on much better conditions than external markets would do. Gaur et al. (2014) confirm that there is synergy in a business group in terms of such resources as technological and marketing capabilities as well as international experience, and in this respect, firms belonging to the business group have a competitive advantage over individual companies. Such synergy is strengthened by good coordination of operating activities within a business group (Chen & Jaw, 2014). This may be supported by the internationalisation of some affiliates (Holmes et al. 2018).

Research shows that Indian business groups undertook "international expansion in order to increase their market coverage and increase competitive advantage" (Ramamurti & Singh, 2009 as cited by Kumar et al., 2012: 187–188). According to Purkayastha et al. (2017), business groups in their international expansion have an advantage over individual firms because as larger organisations by nature, they have a greater propensity to absorb risk and can quickly reap benefits of entering international markets. They are also able to attract more customers from foreign markets and achieve higher international sales than individual companies which give them another advantage (Lamin, 2013).

Shukla and Akbar (2018) confirm in their research that in a business group having strong managerial ties between all firms within the group, the international development of the group's companies is similar. This is possible due to 'exchange' of information and resources among group's affiliates. Strong direct and indirect capital ties within the group have a similar impact (Shukla & Akbar, 2018). Also, Tan and Meyer (2010) confirm the significant impact of managerial resources on the internationalisation of a business group, namely, its direct foreign investments.

One of the areas covered in the research of business groups' internationalisation is the study of the relationship between the concentration of power in family business groups and internationalisation. Research of Shanmugasundaram (2020) shows that groups in which the share of the founding family is lower than 40% undertook foreign direct investment, while in the case of groups where the share of the family is much greater, business groups preferred to stick to exporting, which is a much less risky foreign activity. This is also consistent with Dau et al. (2021). In turn, Karaevli and Yurtoglu (2021) find that the positive and negative influence of family ownership on the internationalisation of the business group alters depending on the life of the family and market changes.

The research of Kumar et al. (2012) shows that together with an increase in product diversification of the entire business group, its tendency to internationalise decreases. This is due to a large internal market of the group and the difficulties in transferring group-specific resources to foreign markets. Similarly, Chari (2013) proves in his research that the lower the diversification of a business group, the higher the FDI flows are. However, in the case of advanced technological resources, internationalisation is possible despite the large diversification of the group. Also, despite the large degree of diversification of the business group, internationalisation is possible if the group can develop new competences based on its previous international experience. The researchers suggest that group companies wishing to internationalise learn from other companies in the group that have already gained such experience. This requires development of appropriate knowledge-sharing mechanisms within the group. Also, Shukla and Akbar (2018) observe that the transfer of resources and information within the business group influences various strategic decisions, including internationalisation. Other researchers also see a positive impact of the knowledge and experience exchange among group affiliates on one another's internationalisation (Guillén, 2003; Lamin, 2013).

Some researchers note that belonging to a business group may limit affiliates in their efforts to internationalise (Mukherjee et al., 2018; Dau et al., 2021). A lot can depend on their position in the group (Purkayasthaa et al., 2018). On the other hand, reputation of the business group may create unique opportunities for affiliates undertaking internationalisation, or sometimes on the contrary (Mukherjee et al., 2018). Shukla and Akbar (2018) note that if the international experience of some affiliates is negative, the flow of information on this subject limited internationalisation decisions of other affiliates. Also, some affiliates undertaking internationalisation may be reluctant to share full information on this topic. This depends on the degree and type of ties between affiliates, as such a situation is unlikely in the case of strong managerial ties. However, such a phenomenon is very likely in financial business groups.

Purkayastha et al. (2017) notice that business groups lower their overall performance with the increase of their international involvement. This is connected to high costs of coordination and control of foreign operations and the frequently occurring business groups' significant diversification. In fact, it is the excessive diversification of the enterprise itself that has a negative impact on its results (Collis & Montgomery, 1997). On the other hand, studies on the financial effectiveness of internationalisation strategies show heterogeneous results although recent studies have more often observed a positive than negative impact of internationalisation on the effectiveness of enterprises (Barłożewski, 2017). This means that achieving good financial results on the international market is not easy. Therefore, it is not surprising that the results of international activities of business groups in the long term may not be the highest.

In this context, results of Pérez-López et al. (2018) research are very interesting, as they show the relationship between ownership, management, organisational culture, and the profitability of business groups established abroad by Spanish companies. This is the first such study known to the author of this chapter, which presents the internationalisation of enterprises (in this case, family enterprises) by creating business groups on a foreign market.

The review of literature on the internationalisation of business groups presented above indicates that this is an important area of international business research. So far, various aspects of the internationalisation of business groups have been studied. One of them is the emergence of coopetition between subsidiaries. Previous studies prove that simultaneous cooperation and competition can be easily traced within international business groups (Luo, 2005; Tippmann et al., 2018). Cooperation often appears in production and R&D and is aimed at surpassing external competitors. Concurrently, competition can arise as strategic domains of business units begin to overlap because of the expansion of subsidiaries. Business group affiliates compete also for central resources, internal clients, power, or position within the business group (Birkinshaw & Lingblad, 2005; Luo, 2005; Tippmann et al., 2018; Lagerström et al., 2021). The compulsion of local adaptation forces foreign subsidiaries to rely more on their strategic resources to compete with local rivals that often maintain strong networks of customers, suppliers, and distributors. Foreign subsidiaries within business groups are then more focused on competition for resources because the support of the parent company reduces the susceptibility to unforeseen situations on the local market and enables growth of subsidiaries. Competition between subsidiaries may be particularly strong when the economic conditions in the host country are unstable. At the same time, subsidiaries cooperate with each other to exchange knowledge about the market or conclude agreements that increase their market power. An example of competition, related to the necessity to adapt to conditions of the host country, is operations of DuPont corporation units located in Chinese coastal areas, such as Shenzhen, Shanghai, and Guangdong. Competition in their case concerns two basic areas. The first is competition for capital and its reinvestments made by the parent company. The second area is competition for technological support of the parent company, which is to enable better adaptation to local conditions (Luo, 2005). Liu, Jiao, and Xia (2019) prove that if there is a network of affiliates operating in one industry and offering similar products in the host country, more intense competition occurs, which concerns both internal resources and external market. This is not observed when in the host country there are even several affiliates from one business group but operating in different industries. Competition between them also occurs, but only in the internal dimension, and not for customers and external market.

Previous studies prove that the history of business groups and implemented internationalisation strategy are very important determinants of internal coopetition. Some researchers note that the internal competition will be much greater if a business group implements a multinational strategy than a global strategy (Phelps & Fuller, 2000; Li & Ferreira, 2003; Luo, 2005). The global strategy reduces the level of competition between subsidiaries due to clearly defined areas and scopes of their activities. On the other hand, the strategy of a multinational integrated network (and transnational) contributes to the growth of interdependence and cooperation of subsidiaries but also to the growth of competition between them due to overlapping markets, interest in the same clients, lack of regional resources, and evaluation of affiliates from the perspective of financial efficiency (Chambers, 2015). The dualism of competition and cooperation is most visible in the transnational strategy (Luo, 2005).

Empirical Findings

The study, which results are presented in the chapter, uses a survey database of 121 business groups in Poland that was drawn from the databases of business groups that a parent company is listed on the Warsaw Stock Exchange. Data were acquired from surveys with top managers of parent companies from randomly selected business groups, Amadeus database and financial statements published by business groups. Information about the research sample and the method is presented in the introduction, while measures of coopetition and coopetition models are elaborated in Chapter 2.

The study sample contained 81 business groups with international scope of operations, which constituted 66.9% of the whole business group sample. Half of those business groups (namely 41) operate within the European Economic Area (EEA), 31 groups indicate that they operate on global markets, and only 9 are concentrated on Central and Eastern Europe (CEE). It is interesting that so many business groups deriving from Poland operate globally now as earlier studies indicate that only small percentage of firms studied operate globally (Jarosiński, 2013), including companies listed on the Warsaw Stock Exchange (Obłój & Wąsowska, 2010).

Below, two variables (scope of operations and area of international operations) are presented against identified coopetition types. Originally, the analysis also included an industry internationalisation level but, in any analysis performed, an industry internationalisation does not have much influence on internationalisation of business groups studied whichever type of coopetition it was paired with.

Coopetition types are identified with the use of two criteria: intensity of competition and cooperation, and direction of coopetition. The intensity of competition and cooperation is measured on 5-point Likert type scale. In the study, four- and nine-field matrix of coopetition is used. In the four-field matrix, the intensity of cooperation and competition is divided into low and high, while in the nine-field matrix is split into low, medium, and high. The second criterium, direction of coopetition, enables to distinguish unidirectional and network coopetition (see Chapter 2).

Table 6.1 presents coopetition types identified based on four-field coopetition matrix versus scope of operations and area of international

Table 6.1 Coopetition types based on four-field coopetition matrix versus scope of operations and area of international operations

Coopetition types	*Scope of operations*		*Area of international operations*		
	National	*International*	*CEE*	*EEA*	*Global*
Low cooperation and competition	12.9%	11.1%	22.2%	12.2%	6.5%
High cooperation and low competition	87.1%	88.9%	77.8%	87.8%	93.5%
Total	100% (N = 31)	100% (N = 81)	100% (N = 9)	100% (N = 41)	100% (N = 31)
Chi-squared test	$p = 0.791; \chi^2 = 0.070$		$p = 0.395; \chi^2 = 1.855$		

Source: Own elaboration.

operations. There are identified only two out of four coopetition types. First relates to low cooperation and competition, while second refers to high cooperation and low competition. There are no major differences between coopetition types, although high cooperation and low competition is slightly more supportive for international scope of operations of business groups in the sample. Within the set of internationalised business groups, high cooperation induces a bit broader scope of international operations, especially the global one. Unfortunately, the chi-squared test does not prove statistically significant differences between groups.

A more careful look at coopetition types is presented in Table 6.2, where coopetition variables are analysed in a more detailed way with the use of nine-field coopetition matrix. In the study, there are identified only five (out of nine) types of coopetition. That was coopetition with: (1) low cooperation and competition, (2) medium cooperation and low competition, (3) medium cooperation and competition, (4) high cooperation and low competition, and (5) high cooperation and medium competition.

In both sets of business groups – operating only within the country and internationally – the most often used coopetition type is high cooperation and low competition (Table 6.2). 61.3% of non-internationalised part of the sample and 66.7% of the internationalised part of the sample fell into this category with a small advantage for internationalised business groups. This may suggest that simultaneous high cooperation and low competition support the international scope of operations of business groups studied. This type of coopetition induces operations rather in the EEA than global or CEE scope of operations. The second most often indicated category is high cooperation and medium competition. Here, differences are smaller with the advantage for business groups operating in the country only.

Table 6.2 Coopetition types based on nine-field coopetition matrix versus scope of operations and area of international operations

Coopetition types	*Scope of operations*		*Area of international operations*		
	National	*International*	*CEE*	*EEA*	*Global*
Low cooperation and competition	3.2%	0.0%	0.0%	0.0%	0.0%
Medium cooperation and low competition	6.5%	8.6%	11.1%	9.8%	6.5%
Medium cooperation and competition	3.2%	2.5%	11.1%	2.4%	0.0%
High cooperation and low competition	61.3%	66.7%	55.6%	73.2%	61.3%
High cooperation and medium competition	25.8%	22.2%	22.2%	14.6%	32.3%
Total	100% (N = 31)	100% (N = 81)	100% (N = 9)	100% (N = 41)	100% (N = 31)
Chi-squared test	$p = 0.555; \chi^2 = 3.018$		$p = 0.339; \chi^2 = 6.811$		

Source: Own elaboration.

Interestingly, among those business groups, ten groups operate globally and six in the EEA. This would very cautiously support the conclusion that moderate competition within a business group may force firms to increase their scope of operations beyond Europe to be more competitive. Another cautious conclusion can be that at least medium cooperation within a business group is required for the group to start internationalisation. Unfortunately, also in this case, the chi-squared test does not prove statistically significant differences between groups.

Table 6.3 presents coopetition types identified based on its direction versus scope of operations and area of international operations. There are no major differences between coopetition types although network coopetition is slightly more supportive for international scope of operations of business groups in the sample. This type of coopetition induces operations rather in the EEA and global than CEE scope of operations. Unfortunately, the chi-squared test does not prove statistically significant differences between business groups and conclusions are drawn carefully.

Table 6.3 Coopetition types based on its direction versus scope of operations and area of international operations

Coopetition types	*Scope of operations*		*Areas of international operations*		
	National	*International*	*CEE*	*EEA*	*Global*
Unidirectional coopetition	9.7%	7.4%	11.1%	7.3%	6.5%
Network coopetition	90.3%	92.6%	88.9%	92.7%	93.5%
Total	100% ($N = 31$)	100% ($N = 81$)	100% ($N = 9$)	100% ($N = 41$)	100% ($N = 31$)
Chi-squared test	$p = 0.693$; $\chi^2 = 0.156$		$p = 0.895$; $\chi^2 = 0.222$		

Source: Own elaboration.

Conclusion

The study constitutes an attempt to understand the relationship between coopetition within business groups and their internationalisation, aspiring to contribute to the international business as well to coopetition literature.

First, data indicate that when there is high cooperation within a business group and, at the same time, there is low to medium internal competition, slightly more business groups have tendency to internationalise their scope of operations. This is in line with Gaur et al. (2014) who state that synergy within a business group helps achieve better strategic results, and Chen and Jaw (2014) who stress that such synergy is reinforced by good internal group coordination. Internal cooperation through a network of managerial ties within a group and its impact on groups' internationalisation is emphasised by Tan & Meyer (2010) and Shukla and Akbar (2018). Other researchers also note a positive influence of internal cooperation of business groups affiliates on their internationalisation (Guillén, 2003; Lamin, 2013). At the same time, it is line with observations of Crick and Crick (2021) that business cooperating a lot with one another on their national market increase competition against one another in international markets. Additionally, low intensity of competition within an international business group could be a strong incentive to improve subsidiaries' performance (Birkinshaw & Lingblad, 2005; Luo, 2005).

It is also noted in the study that despite high internal cooperation too much internal competition could negatively affect internationalisation. This is in line with the observations of Dau et al. (2021) that in some business groups' affiliates may be hampered in their efforts to internationalise. Also, Shukla and Akbar (2018) note that in some business groups the exchange of information may be limited, and this in fact may happen due to internal competition.

Another finding in this study is that network coopetition slightly supports the internationalisation of business groups. This is, in turn, consistent with Chen and Jaw (2014), who prove in their research that the strong network of connections existing in a business group positively influences the increase in the internationalisation degree of the parent company. Also, Feiyang et al. (2022) notice that if firms create coopetition networks in their country, they can easily extend this network beyond its borders. At the same time, network coopetition supports internationalisation of business groups to more distant areas than CEE.

This study has some limitations. The first limitation worth mentioning is that only the perspective of the parent company is considered in this study. The second limitation is the sparse number of variables considered, which do not allow for a more sophisticated statistical analysis. However, the study refers to an important area of international business research that requires further investigation. In the future, the study should be repeated in other countries to make sure that the local environment does not influence the study results. Also, in future studies, the perspective of business group subsidiaries could be considered as in this study coopetition within a business group is perceived from the perspective of the parent company only.

References

Aguilera, R.V., Crespí-Cladera, R., Infantes, P.M. & Pascual-Fuster, B. (2020). Business groups and internationalisation: Effective identification and future agenda. *Journal of World Business*, 55(4), 1–17.

Barłożewski, K. (2017). *Wpływ ekspansji zagranicznej na efektywność przedsiębiorstw [Influence of foreign expansion on the efficiency of enterprises]*. Warszawa: C.H. Beck.

Birkinshaw, J. & Lingblad, M. (2005). Intrafirm competition and charter evolution in the multibusiness firm. *Organization Science*, 16(6), 674–686.

Carney, M., Van Essen, M., Estrin, S. & Shapiro, D. (2017). Business group prevalence and impact across countries and over time: What can we learn from the literature? *Multinational Business Review*, 25(1), 52–76.

Chambers, M. (2015). *Dynamic, inter-subsidiary relationships of competition and collaboration*, Doctoral Dissertation, Cranfield University.

Chari, M.D.R. (2013). Business groups and foreign direct investments by developing country firms: An empirical test in India. *Journal of World Business*, 48(3), 349–359.

Chen, Y.Y. & Jaw, Y.-L. (2014). How do business groups' small world networks effect diversification, innovation, and internationalization? *Asia Pacific Journal of Management*, 31(4), 1019–1044.

Collis, D.J. & Montgomery, C.A. (1997). *Corporate strategy: Resources and the scope of the firm*. Chicago, IL: McGraw Hill.

Crick, J.M. & Crick, D. (2021). The yin and yang nature of coopetition activities: Non-linear effects and the moderating role of competitive intensity for internationalised firms. *International Marketing Review*, 38(4), 690–716.

Dau, L.A., Morck, R. & Yeung, B. (2021). Business groups and the study of international business: A Coasean synthesis and extension. *Journal of International Business Studies*, 52(2), 161–211.

Feiyang, G., Tienan, W., Linbing, S. & Liqing, T. (2022). The synergistic effect of ego-network stability and whole network position: A perspective of transnational coopetition network. *Journal of Enterprise Information Management*, 35(3), 847–865.

Gaur, A.S., Kumar, V. & Singh, D. (2014). Institutions, resources, and internationalization of emerging economy firms. *Journal of World Business*, 49(1), 12–20.

Holmes Jr., R.M., Hoskisson, R.E., Kim, H., Wan, W.P. & Holcomb, T.R. (2018). International strategy and business groups: A review and future research agenda. *Journal of World Business*, 53(2), 134–150.

Jarosiński, M. (2013). *Procesy i modele internacjonalizacji polskich przedsiębiorstw [Processes and models of internationalisation of Polish enterprises]*. Warszawa: Oficyna Wydawnicza SGH.

Karaevli, A. & Yurtoglu, B.B. (2021). Family ownership, market development, and internationalization of Turkish business groups (1925–2017). *Journal of World Business*, 56(6), 1–17.

Kumar, V., Gaur, A.S. & Pattnaik, Ch. (2012). Product diversification and international expansion of business groups: Evidence from India. *Management International Review*, 52(2), 175–192.

Lagerström, K., Leite, E. & Pahlberg, C. (2021). *Cooperating while competing in multinational corporations*, in Arora-Jonsson, S., Brunsson, N., Hasse, R. & Lagerström, K. (eds.) *Competition: What it is and why it happens*. New York: Oxford University Press.

Lamin, A. (2013). Business groups as information resource: An investigation of business group affiliation in the Indian software services industry. *Academy of Management Journal*, 56(5), 1487–1509.

Li D., Ferreira M. (2003), *Technology transfer within MNEs: An investigation of inter-subsidiary competition and cooperation*. Paper presented at the 4th IB Research Forum at Temple University, Philadelphia, 29 March 2003.

Liu, Y., Jiao, J. & Xia J. (2019). Subsidiary networks and foreign subsidiary performance: A coopetition perspective. *Management and Organization Review*, 15(1), 111–143.

Luo, Y. (2005). Toward coopetition within a multinational enterprise: A perspective from foreign subsidiaries. *Journal of World Business*, 40(1), 71–90.

Mukherjee, D., Makarius, E.E. & Stevens, Ch.E. (2018). Business group reputation and affiliates' internationalization strategies. *Journal of World Business*, 53(2), 93–103.

Obłój, K., Wąsowska, A. (2010). *Uwarunkowania strategii umiędzynarodowienia polskich firm giełdowych [Determinants of the internationalisation strategy of Polish listed companies]*, in Krupski, R. (ed.) *Zarządzanie strategiczne. Strategie organizacji [Strategic management. Organisation strategies]*. Wałbrzych: Prace Naukowe WWSZiP.

Pérez-López, M.C., Gómez-Miranda, M.E., Argente-Linares, E. & López-Sánchez, L. (2018). The internationalisation of Spanish family firms through business groups: Factors affecting the profitability, and the moderating effect of the family nature of the Spanish business. *Revista de Contabilidad – Spanish Accounting Review*, 21(1), 82–90.

Phelps, N. & Fuller, C. (2000). Multinationals, intracorporate competition and regional development. *Economic Geography*, 76(3), 224–243.

Purkayastha, S., Kumar, V. & Lu, J.W. (2017). Business group heterogeneity and the internationalization-performance relationship: Evidence from Indian business groups. *Asia Pacific Journal of Management*, 34(2), 247–279.

Purkayasthaa, S., Manolova, T.S. & Edelman, L.F. (2018). Business group effects on the R&D intensity-internationalization relationship: Empirical evidence from India. *Journal of World Business*, 53(2), 104–117.

Shanmugasundaram, S. (2020). Internationalization and governance of Indian family-owned business groups. *Journal of Family Business Management*, 10(1), 76–94.

Shukla, D.M. & Akbar, M. (2018). Diffusion of internationalization in business group networks: Evidence from India. *Management Decision*, 56(2), 406–420.

Tan, D. & Meyer, K.E. (2010). Business groups' outward FDI: A managerial resources perspective. *Journal of International Management*, 16(2), 154–164.

Tippmann, E., Scott, P. S., Reilly, M. & O'Brien, D. (2018). Subsidiary coopetition competence: Navigating subsidiary evolution in the multinational corporation. *Journal of World Business*, 53(4), 540–554.

7 Coopetition and Corporate Governance within Business Groups

Maria Aluchna

Introduction

Corporate governance is understood as mechanisms and institutions which provide an effective structure of management and control over firms (Monks & Minow, 2004). The term addresses both the institutional setting with political system, regulation, and social norms as well as checks and balances set-up at the company level (Tricker, 2012). Corporate governance has been dominated by the paradigm of creating shareholder value with its utmost goal to protect investor rights, yet in recent years scholars and practitioners have shifted the focus towards creating long-term sustainable value integrating stakeholders and shareholder expectations and improving financial as well as ESG performance (Mallin, 2004; Zattoni & Cuomo, 2008; Cuomo et al., 2016; Edmans, 2020).

While corporate governance traditionally has public listed companies in its spotlight, there is growing interest in adopting its framework for other types of organisations, including complex business groups (Ahmed & Uddin, 2018; Sanan et al., 2019), which are an organisational and legal form of economic activity prevalent around the world (Perkins et al., 2014; Jansson & Larsson-Olaison, 2015; Colli & Colpan, 2016; Poczter, 2018). The nature and focus of corporate governance appear to differ in business groups as compared to standalone companies (Hsieh et al., 2010) driven by the business group's organisational complexity, density of network relationships, number of affiliated companies, multi-layer ownership structure, and diversification strategy across different market segments (Gleason et al., 2012). Specifically, the ownership structure appears to be a distinct corporate governance mechanism having significant impact on the business group's activity. Business groups show a dominance of the controlling entity (founder, family, or fund) and tend to adopt various solutions of disproportionate ownership and leveraged control, including dual-class shares, pyramidal structures, and company by-laws increasing the voting power of the controlling shareholder (Masulis et al., 2011; Ahmed & Uddin, 2018; Chung & Zhu, 2021). Such solutions add to the vertical links across the business group and increase the hierarchy of decision-making and control, which is additionally strengthened by

DOI: 10.4324/9781003324775-8

interlocking directorates between the parent company and affiliated firms (Yiu et al., 2007; Lee & Hooy, 2018). Interlocking directorates take the form of a personnel union between directors and executives to centralise decision-making. The parent company coordinates the activities across the group, leaving little autonomy to affiliated firms (Luo, 2005; Poczter, 2018). While concentrated ownership and control increase the overall unanimity of decision-making, improve coordination, and add to procedure cohesion in business groups (Chung & Zhu, 2021), it may also be detrimental for the group, limiting its ability of change and adapting to the new market environment. Concentrated ownership and control are likely to discourage group decision-makers from cooperation between affiliated companies in the form of knowledge exchange or coopetition.

The study examines the intensity of intra-group coopetition in business groups regarding their selected features. Specifically, the study concentrates on the relations between the intensity of intra-group coopetition and concentrated control, interlocking directorate's policy, the adoption of group procedures, the type of dominant investor, and the role of the parent company. To verify assumed relations, Poland was purposefully chosen, which is a country showing corporate governance based on hierarchies with weak external control mechanisms (Berglöf & Claessens 2006; Hardi & Buti, 2012), where listed companies reveal high-ownership concentration (Aluchna & Kamiński, 2017).

Theoretical Lenses

Corporate governance offers a set of rules and principles assuring equitable rights of all shareholders, who are encouraged to actively participate in shareholder meetings exercising their voting and decision-making power (OECD, 2015) in an environment of high transparency standards and protection of investor rights. Detailed guidelines refer to the functioning and the composition of the board, formation of specialised board committees, directors' duties based on the accountability and responsibility to shareholders and stakeholders as well as to the practice of executive compensation referring to the pay size and structure, bonuses, and incentive programmes (Zattoni & Cuomo, 2008; Cuomo et al., 2016).

This set of rules and principles also covers the nature of corporate governance in business groups; although considering their organisational complexity and ownership pattern, the concerns are differently distributed (Zattoni, 1999; Chung & Luo, 2008; Sanan et al., 2019). While the term "business group" remains ubiquitous in the economics and management literature, it is generally understood as a collection of heterogeneous companies tied with formal and informal links (Pursey et al., 2007). Formal links are represented by ownership, common administrative or financial control, and stable contractual relationships (Guillen, 2000;

Cuervo-Cazzura, 2006). The informal links in the form of interpersonal trust, personal interlockings, social ties, ethical and religious similarities, as well as shared commercial backgrounds, reinforce financial and organisational linkages amongst affiliated companies (Morck & Yeung, 2010; Mitra & Pattanayak, 2013).

Corporate governance in business groups is challenged by two competing frameworks that are employed to understand group's emergence and evolution (Carney et al., 2018). Firstly, corporate governance focuses on the coordination role to achieve synergy effects offered by the business group environment. Business groups, as opposed to standalone firms (Hsieh et al., 2010), offer a specific organisation setting and create a network of affiliated companies to exploit numerous benefits of sharing resources, coordinated diversification and investment strategies, advantages of substantial size, scope and market share, as well as position and political connectedness (Villalonga, 2004; Hsieh et al., 2010; Chung & Zhu, 2021). In a sense, business group settings enable avoiding negative consequences of institutional voids reducing uncertainty, enhancing trust, providing access to financing, and overcoming market frictions (Fisman & Khanna, 2004; Selekler-Goksen & Öktem, 2009; Mahmood et al., 2013; Meuer & Backes-Gellner, 2015). As noted by Carney et al. (2018: 498), business groups "are viewed as a functional response to an underdeveloped institutional context, and one that enhances the economic performance of affiliated firms", which may explain the role and prevalence of business groups in emerging markets (Claessens & Yurtoglu, 2012). Yet, corporate governance is also challenged by a darker side of business groups, which indicates that their benefits are achieved by rent-seeking owners at the expense of minority shareholders and society (Claessens et al., 2000; Claessens et al., 2002; Bozec et al., 2010; Bena & Ortiz-Molina, 2013; Buchuk, et al., 2014). Business groups are often governed by controlling shareholders who use the mechanism of disproportionate ownership to leverage control. For instance, controlling owners adopt a pyramidal structure that consists of several companies, with the main listed company located at its apex and linked by multiple layers of ownership relations (Zattoni, 1999; Bennedsen & Nielsen, 2006, 2010) strengthen by cross shareholdings and mutual capital interdependencies (Patel et al., 2002; Perkins et al., 2014). Through the resulting chain of arrangements, portfolio companies and financial vehicles are directly and indirectly controlled, governed, and monitored by the ultimate owner (Bertrand et al., 2002) who tend to engage in related party transactions to extract private benefits and to expropriate minority investors. Those problems may lead to tunnelling defined as channelling "resources away from firms in which the controlling shareholder has low cash flow rights toward firms in which they have high cash flow rights" (Buchuk et al., 2014: 190) and are exacerbated in the context of weak institutional environment and insufficient investor protection.

In addition, business groups include the management of relations between the parent company and affiliated firms and amongst affiliated firms (Song et al., 2016). The links determine the nature of activity of the parent company and its subsidiaries regarding control, cooperation, and competition (Becker-Ritterspach & Dörrenbächer, 2011). For instance, intra-group links represent the control and coordination of resources, competences, and actions undertaken for the purpose of achieving group goals. The horizontal connectedness refers to ties between affiliated companies and is viewed as the intensity of internal transactions and cross subsidisation, cross shareholdings, interlocking directorates, and social relations (Lee & Hooy, 2018; Oh et al., 2018). The relations between affiliated companies and the parent company or the owner illustrate vertical links and take the form of vertical ownership and control concentration, as well as the role of the dominant owner in the management and ownership portfolio (Yiu et al., 2007). As outlined in a Deloitte report (2013), subsidiaries present an interesting set of corporate governance challenges and dilemmas. This is a classic attempt to keep the balance between the degree of control that needs to be exercised by the parent company over its subsidiaries and the degree of autonomy that needs to be provided to them to enjoy the advantages of cooperation, exchange of resources, and achieving synergy effects (Yiu et al., 2007). Subsidiary governance in a business group is also an issue of standardisation, systems, and procedures across the whole entity and the process of cascading principles and values from the level of shareholders, board, and parent company towards local adaptation at subsidiary level.

The business group setting is a natural environment for coopetition between affiliated companies. Coopetition is defined as simultaneous competition and cooperation among firms with the purpose to create value (Tidström & Rajala, 2016; Gnyawali & Charleton, 2018). Firstly, affiliated firms cooperate within a group sharing group recourses such as infrastructure, brand, customer base, funds, exchange know-how and experience, and rotating managerial teams (Hsieh et al., 2010; Yaprak & Karademir, 2010; Chabowski et al., 2018). Yet, affiliated firms compete for access to these resources, often paying fees to the parent company. Particularly, fierce competition is noted within the group investment policy when the parent company decides about the distribution of funds via the internal capital market and chooses projects in which the group intends to invest (Stein, 1997). Secondly, while affiliated firms enjoy the advantage of an internal market which reduces risk and transaction costs and secures contract enforcement (Mishra & Akbar, 2007; Kim & Lui, 2015), they also compete to participate in a commercial agreement offering products and services. Hence, firms face paradoxical tension of coopetition strategy, which assumes that a simultaneous combination of competition and cooperation between subsidiaries and affiliated firms (Dahl, 2014; Tidström, 2014), using formal and informal coordination, leaves them striving to manage coopetitive goals (Seran et al., 2016).

While the negative consequences of business groups relate to the expropriation of minority investors and exploitation of political connections for rent seeking at the cost of the whole society is extensively studied (Bena & Ortiz-Molina, 2013; Buchuk, et al., 2014), it can be argued that the dominance of strong control and vertical links may be detrimental for the development of inter-group coopetition. The strong vertical links of affiliated firms with the parent company and tight control by the dominant shareholder may reduce the horizontal relations of coopetition. Amongst the shareholder types, industry investors who operate within large international business groups appear to have the strongest control over affiliated companies. Thus, it can be assumed that there is a negative association between intra-group coopetition intensity and concentrated control by the dominant shareholder. In addition, the industry investor is expected to lower intra-group coopetition intensity. Since the presence of shared group procedures connects affiliated firms and increases group cohesion and can limit horizontal cooperative links, it is also likely to lower intra-group coopetition intensity.

Unlike vertical ownership links relations based on interlocking directorates, which offer a personnel union between executives and decision-makers of affiliated firms and the parent company, are more flexible and focus on experience exchange. It can be assumed that personal interlocks enhance coopetition between group members and stimulate intra-group coopetition intensity. Finally, it can be argued that the role of the parent company is likely to be associated with the willingness of group members to cooperate and compete. Specifically, the investment role of the parent company shifts decision-making at the top levels of the group and limits the horizontal relations between affiliated forms, whereas the coordination role of the parent company is likely to stimulate intra-group coopetition.

Empirical Findings

The study, which results are presented in the chapter, uses a survey database of 121 business groups in Poland that was drawn from the databases of business groups that a parent company is listed on the Warsaw Stock Exchange. Data were acquired from surveys with top managers of parent companies from randomly selected business groups, Amadeus database and financial statements published by business groups. Information about the research sample and method is presented in the introduction, while measures of coopetition and coopetition types are elaborated in Chapter 2.

The chapter investigates the relationship between coopetition and ownership structure (the presence of a majority shareholder), type of dominant shareholder, role of the parent company, existence of a personnel union at the executive level, and presence of procedures at group level. It also collects information on the number of subsidiaries and the number of organisational levels which serve as control variables. The set of variables used in the analysis is presented in Table 7.1.

Table 7.1 Variables used in the analysis

Variable	*Definition*
Intra-group coopetition intensity	Binary variable – 0 for low intra-group coopetition intensity (low cooperation and competition) and 1 for high intra-group coopetition intensity (high cooperation and low competition)
Majority shareholder	Binary variable – 0 for lack of a majority shareholder (no shareholder with more than 50% of votes), 1 for the presence of a majority shareholder (more than 50% of votes)
Type of dominant shareholder	The identification of the dominant shareholder based on the following coding: 1 – industry shareholder 2 – individual investor 3 – financial investor 4 – state
Role of the parent company	The identification of the dominant shareholder based on the following coding: 1 – investment role – the parent company decides about acquisitions and sales of subsidiaries 2 – investment role – the parent company decides about the distribution of funds for investment in subsidiaries 3 – coordination role – the parent company manages resources in subsidiaries 4 – coordination role – the parent company facilitates cooperation between subsidiaries 5 – coordination role – the parent company divides the production process amongst subsidiaries
Interlocking directorates at executive level	Binary variable – 0 for the lack of interlocking directorates at executive level, 1 for the presence of interlocking directorates at executive level
Procedures at group level	Binary variable – 0 for the lack of the procedures at group level, 1 for the presence of the procedures at group level
Number of subsidiaries	Binary variable – 0 for the total number of subsidiaries in the business group at 30 or below and 1 for the total number of subsidiaries in the business group above 30
Number of organisational levels	Total number of organisational levels in the business group

Source: Own elaboration.

Considering the nature of variables, the chi-squared analysis is adopted to find the relationships between the coopetition type and selected corporate governance characteristics.

Descriptive statistics for variables used in the analysis are presented in Table 7.2, whereas the frequencies for the role of the parent company, the type of dominant shareholder, and the type of dominant shareholder and number of organisational levels are shown in Table 7.3.

Table 7.2 Descriptive statistics for coopetition type and corporate governance characteristics

Variable	*Mean*	*SD*	*Mix*	*Max*
Intra-group coopetition intensity	0.876	0.331	0	1
Majority shareholder	0.429	0.497	0	1
Interlocking directorates at executive level	0.702	0.459	0	1
Procedures at group level	0.843	0.365	0	1
Number of subsidiaries	15.06	23.84	1	196
Number of organisational levels	2.48	0.76	1	5

Source: Own elaboration.

Table 7.3 Frequencies of the role of the parent company, the type of dominant shareholder, and number of organisational levels

Variable	*Frequencies*	*Percentage*	*Cumulative percentage*
Parent role			
Investment role	83	69%	69%
Investment role – the parent company decides about acquisitions and sales of subsidiaries	53	44%	44%
Investment role – the parent company decides about the distribution of funds for investment in subsidiaries	30	25%	69%
Coordination role	38	31%	100%
Coordination role – the parent company manages resources in subsidiaries	8	7%	76%
Coordination role – the parent company facilitates cooperation between subsidiaries	4	3%	79%
Coordination role – the parent company divides the production process amongst subsidiaries	26	21%	100%
Dominant shareholder type			
Industry investor	39	33%	33%
Individual investor	53	45%	78%
Financial investor	19	16%	94%
State	7	9%	100%

Source: Own elaboration.

Descriptive statistics reveal that 87% of business groups in the sample pursue coopetition of high intensity of cooperation and low intensity of competition. In nearly 43% of business groups analysed, there is a majority shareholder who owns over 50% of votes. Interlocking directorates in the form of a personnel union take place in 70% of business groups, whereas common procedures function in 84% at group level. Additionally, business groups sampled differ in terms of size measured by the number of firms ranging between 1 and 196 and the number of levels of business group ranging between 1 and 5; on average, there are 15 subsidiaries and 2 organisational levels in sampled business groups.

Table 7.3 shows that the investment role, when the parent company decides about acquisitions and sales of subsidiaries and the distribution of funds for investment in subsidiaries, is the most common role of the parent company amongst the business groups analysed. In 45% of business groups sampled, the individual investor is the largest shareholder, followed by industry investors, which remains consistent with the overall characteristics of Polish corporate governance (Aluchna & Kamiński, 2017).

The next step in the research process was to test the link between intra-group coopetition intensity and control mechanisms, such as the presence of the majority shareholder in the ownership structure. The results of the chi-squared test are presented in Table 7.4.

Table 7.4 reveals that the link between intra-group coopetition intensity and the presence of the majority shareholder is statistically significant. Specifically, higher coopetition is observed in the case of dispersed ownership when the largest shareholder holds 50% of votes or less.

Next, it was tested if the presence of an industry investor as the dominant shareholders is associated with lower intra-group coopetition intensity. The results are shown in Table 7.5.

The results reported in Table 7.5 show that the relationship between the intra-group coopetition intensity and the type of largest shareholder remains weakly statistically significant at the tendency level. The evidence shows that high coopetition takes place in business groups that are governed by individual investors. Business groups showing low intra-group coopetition intensity are dominated by industry investors.

The analysis of the relation between the adoption of group procedures and the intra-group coopetition intensity does not reveal any statistically significant results. Further to the above, the role of interlocking directorates in the form of a personnel union at the executive level in the business

Table 7.4 Intra-group coopetition intensity and majority shareholder

Intra-group coopetition intensity	*No majority shareholder*	*Presence of majority shareholder*	*Total*
Low	5 (33.33%)	10 (66.67%)	15 (100%)
High	64 (60.38%)	42 (39.62%)	106 (100%)
Total	69 (57.02%)	52 (42.98%)	121 (100%)

Source: Own elaboration.
$p < 0.05$; $\chi^2 = 3.92$.

Table 7.5 Intra-group coopetition intensity and type of the dominant shareholder

Intra-group coopetition intensity	*Industry investor*	*Individual investor*	*Financial investor*	*State*	*Total*
Low	8 (57.14%)	3 (21.43%)	3 (21.43%)	0 (0%)	14 (100%)
High	31 (39.81%)	50 (48.08%)	16 (15.38%)	7 (6.73%)	104 (100%)
Total	39 (33.05%)	53 (44.92%)	19 (16.10%)	7 (5.73%)	118 (100%)

Source: Own elaboration.
$p = 0.1$; $\chi^2 = 5.96$.

Table 7.6 Intra-group coopetition intensity and interlocking directorates

Intra-group coopetition intensity	*No personnel union*	*Presence of personnel union*	*Total*
Low	7 (46.67%)	8 (53.33%)	15 (100%)
High	29 (27.36%)	77 (72.64%)	106 (100%)
Total	36 (29.75%)	85 (70.25%)	121 (100%)

Source: Own elaboration.
$p = 0.1$; $\chi^2 = 2.34$.

group was investigated. The results of the chi-squared test are presented in Table 7.6.

As shown in Table 7.6, the relationship between intra-group coopetition intensity and the presence of a personnel union at the executive level remains weakly statistically significant at the tendency level. The evidence shows that high coopetition takes place in business groups which do not introduce a personnel union on the top organisational positions.

Finally, the link between intra-group coopetition intensity and the role of the parent company was verified. The results are presented in Table 7.7.

Table 7.7 shows that there is a statistically significant relationship between the intra-group coopetition intensity and the role of the parent company. Specifically, business groups showing low coopetition have parent companies focusing on a coordination role, dividing the production process amongst subsidiaries. In business groups of high coopetition, the parent company plays an investment role and decides about acquisitions and sales of subsidiaries.

To sum up, findings of the study give an interesting insight into relation between corporate governance mechanisms and coopetition. First, it is

Table 7.7 Intra-group coopetition intensity and the role of the parent company

Intra-group coopetition intensity	*Investment role (acquisition/ sales of subsidiaries)*	*Investment role (distribution of funds)*	*Coordination role (managing resources)*	*Coordination role (cooperation between subsidiaries)*	*Coordination role (dividing production)*	*Total*
Low	8 (53.33%)	0 (0%)	0 (0%)	1 (6.67%)	6 (40%)	15 (100%)
High	45 (42.45%)	30 (28.30%)	8 (7.55%)	3 (2.83%)	20 (18.87%)	106 (100%)
Total	53 (43.80%)	30 (24.79%)	8 (6.61%)	4 (3.31%)	26 (21.49)	121 (100%)

Source: Own elaboration.
$p < 0.1$; $\chi^2 = 8.39$.

shown that certain corporate governance features may block the business group's ability to increase cooperation and competition between subsidiaries, which may, in turn, affect the ability to respond to market dynamics. This is particularly significant for the patterns of ownership structure – the presence of a dominant shareholder and the presence of an industry investor as the dominant shareholder. As those two solutions increase control (Schnyder, 2012), they may at the same time limit the flexibility of subsidiaries and discourage intra-group coopetition. On the other hand, results show that the presence of a personnel union in the form interlocking directorate's policies between subsidiaries constitutes an environment for intra-group coopetition. In addition, in business groups of high coopetition, the parent company plays an active role focusing on investment activity and decides about acquisitions and sales of subsidiaries. These results can be interpreted as evidence of a trade-off between control via ownership mechanisms and the flexibility and activity of subsidiaries. Second, the results help understand the functioning of business groups and the link between corporate governance characteristics and intra-group coopetition in the context of a less industrialised economy (Poczter, 2018). As noted by Meuer and Backes-Gellner (2015), business groups adapt to persist in layers of co-existing corporate systems and are found to develop multiple equilibria, which are responses to a different institutional environment (Fainshmidt et al., 2018). Thus, findings may suggest that while given corporate governance patterns have emerged in the Polish environment known for its concentrated ownership, insufficient investor protection, and the dominance of hierarchies over markets and are efficient to secure control over business groups' recourse, they may at the same time be detrimental for further development, limiting the potential of business groups to engage in networks, intra-organisational relations, and coopetition.

Conclusion

Coopetition offers a new approach to strategic responses in the context of a dynamically changing environment and competition landscape, as well as offers new settings to form and develop intra-organisational relations and networks (Dahl, 2014; Seran et al., 2016). Scholars have identified determinants of coopetition pointing at the requirement of a specific organisational and environmental context (Birkinshaw & Lingblad, 2005). This study intends to add to this literature by investigating the intensity of intra-organisational coopetition in business groups focusing on selected aspects of corporate governance.

The comparative analysis indicates a uniqueness of business groups in relation to standalone firms and multi-divisional companies (Hsieh et al., 2010; Gleason et al., 2012). Business groups pursue a diversification strategy via many subsidiaries, which function under common ownership and legal control and cooperate for common goals (Khanna & Yafeh, 2007). With the need to coordinate actions of numerous subsidiaries, functioning of an internal market, and different directions for development, business groups can be distinguished by their management based on ownership hierarchies and decision-making by the parent company (Poczter, 2018).

The study shows the relationships between intra-group coopetition intensity and selected corporate governance features. Specifically, it focuses on the importance of the presence of a dominant (controlling) shareholder, the presence of an industry investor as the dominant shareholder, the adoption of common procedures at group level, the interlocking directorate's policy, and the role of the parent company distinguishing between investment versus coordination roles. Results show that concentration of control and the presence of an industry investor as the dominant shareholder are negatively associated with the intensity of coopetition. In addition, the interlocking directorate's policy and the investment role of the parent company are positively linked with the intensity of coopetition. The adoption of universal procedures at the group level is statistically insignificant for the intensity of intra-group coopetition. While results suggest that concentrated ownership and the dominant role of the industry investor in a business group may appear to be an optimal choice in the context of insufficient investor protection and hierarchical control system, these mechanisms may constrain the development of intra-group coopetition.

Results should, nevertheless, be treated with some degree of caution due to some limitations in the sample and focusing on one country. These findings open new opportunities for further research. Studies on a larger number of countries, with a consideration of different ownership patterns and group cohesion policies in various institutional frameworks, would be an interesting direction for future research and would help understand the interactions between the complex structure of business groups and cooperation relationships between subsidiaries.

References

Ahmed, S. & Uddin, S. (2018). Toward a political economy of corporate governance change and stability in family business groups A morphogenetic approach. *Accounting, Auditing & Accountability Journal*, 31(8), 2192–2217.

Aluchna. M. & Kamiński, B. (2017). Ownership structure and company performance: A panel study from Poland. *Baltic Journal of Management*, 12(4), 485–502.

Becker-Ritterspach, F. & Dörrenbächer, C. (2011). An organizational politics perspective on intra-firm competition in multinational corporations. *Management International Review*, 51(4), 533–559.

Bena, J. & Ortiz-Molina, H. (2013). Pyramidal ownership and the creation of new firms. *Journal of Financial Economics*, 108(3), 798–821.

Bennedsen, M. & Nielsen, K. (2006). *The principle of proportional ownership, investors protection and firm value in Western Europe*. ECGI Working Paper No. 134.

Bennedsen, M. & Nielsen, K. (2010). Incentive and entrenchment effects in European ownership. *Journal of Banking Finance*, 34(9), 2212–2229.

Berglöf, E. & Claessens, S. (2006) Enforcement and good corporate governance in developing countries and transition economies. *World Bank Research Observer*, 21(1), 123–150.

Bertrand, M., Mehta, P. & Mullainathan, S. (2002). Ferreting out tunnelling: An application to Indian business groups. *Quarterly Journal Economics*, 117, 121–148.

Birkinshaw, J. & Lingblad, M. (2005). Intrafirm competition and charter evolution in the multibusiness firm. *Organization Science*, 16(6), 674–686.

Bozec, Y., Bozec, R. & Dia, M. (2010). Overall governance, firm value and deviation from one share-one vote principle. *International Journal of Managerial Finance*, 6(4), 305–328.

Buchuk, D., Larrain, F., Muñoz, F. & Urzúa, F. (2014). The internal capital markets of business groups: Evidence from intra-group loans. *Journal of Financial Economics*, 112(2), 190–212.

Carney, M., Van Essen, M., Estrin, S. & Shapiro, D. (2018). Business Groups reconsidered: Beyond paragons and parasites. *Academy of Management Perspectives*, 32(4), 493–451.

Chabowski, B., Kekec, P., Morgan, N. & Hult, G.T. (2018). An assessment of the exporting literature: Using theory and data to identify future research directions. *Journal of International Marketing*, 26, 118–143.

Chung, C.N. & Zhu, H. (2021). Corporate governance dynamics of political tie formation in emerging economies: Business group affiliation, family ownership, and institutional transition. *Corporate Governance. An International Review*, 29, 381–401.

Chung, Ch.-N. & Luo, X. (2008). Institutional logics or agency costs: The influence of corporate models on business group restructuring in emerging economies. *Organization Science*, 19(5), 766–784.

Claessens, S., Djankov, S., Fan, J.P.H. & Lang, H.P. (2002). Disentangling the incentive and entrenchment effects of large shareholdings. *Journal of Finance*, 57, 2741–2771.

Claessens, S., Diankov, S. & Lang, H. (2000). The separation of ownership and control in East Asian corporation. *Journal of Finance*, 58, 81–112.

Claessens, S. & Yurtoglu, B. (2012). Corporate governance in emerging markets: A survey. *Emerging Market Review*, 15, 1–33.

Colli, A. & Colpan, A. (2016). Business groups and corporate governance: Review, synthesis, and extension. *Corporate Governance. An International Review*, 24(3), 274–302.

Cuervo-Cazzura, A. (2006). Business groups and their types. *Asia Pacific Journal of Management*, 23, 419–437.

Cuomo, F., Mallin, Ch. & Zattoni, A. (2016) Corporate governance codes: A review and research agenda. *Corporate Governance. An International Review*, 24(3), 222–241.

Dahl, J. (2014). Conceptualizing coopetition as a process. An outline of change on cooperative and competitive interactions. *Industrial Marketing Management*, 43, 272–279.

Deloitte (2013). Governance of subsidiaries: A survey of global companies, https://www2.deloitte.com/content/dam/Deloitte/in/Documents/risk/Corporate%20Governance/in-gc-governance-of-subsidiaries-a-survey-of-global-companies-noexp.pdf (Accessed: 1 September 2021).

Edmans, A. (2020). *Grow the pie*. Cambridge: Cambridge University Press.

Fainshmidt, S., Judge, W.Q., Aguilera, R.V. & Smith, A. (2018). Varieties of institutional systems: A contextual taxonomy of understudied countries. *Journal of World Business*, 53(3), 307–322.

Fisman, R. & Khanna, T. (2004). Facilitating development: The role of business groups. *Word Development*, 32(4), 609–628.

Gleason, K.C., Kim, I., Kim, Y.H. & Kim, Y.S. (2012). Corporate governance and diversification. *Asia-Pacific Journal of Financial Studies*, 41, 1–31.

Gnyawali, D.R. & Charleton, T.R. (2018). Nuances in the interplay of competition and cooperation: Towards a theory of coopetition. *Journal of Management*, 44(7), 2511–2534.

Guillen, M. (2000). Business groups in emerging economies: A resourced based view. *Academy of Management Journal*, 43(3), 362–380.

Hardi, P. & Buti, K. (2012). Corporate governance variables: Lessons from a holistic approach to Central-Eastern European practice. *Corporate Governance*, 12, 101–117.

Hsieh, T.-J., Yeh, R.S. & Chen, Y.-J. (2010). Business groups characteristics and affiliated from innovation: The case of Taiwan. *Industrial Marketing Management*, 39, 560–576.

Jansson, A. & Larsson-Olaison, U. (2015). I heard it through the grapevine: Market control of controlling family shareholders. *Corporate Governance: An International Review*, 23(6), 504–551.

Khanna, T. & Yafeh, Y. (2007). Business groups in emerging markets: Paragons or parasites? *Journal of Economic Literature*, 45(2), 331–372.

Kim, Y. & Lui, S. (2015). The impacts of external network and business group on innovation: Do the types of innovation matter? *Journal of Business Research*, 68, 1964–1973.

Lee, K.T. & Hooy, Ch-W. (2018). Can informal corporate governance mechanisms mitigate diversification discount? Evidence from Malaysia. *International Journal of Managerial Finance*, 14(5), 522–541.

Luo, Y. (2005). Toward coopetition within a multinational enterprise: A perspective from foreign subsidiaries. *Journal of World Business*, 40(1), 71–90.

Mahmood, I.P., Chung, C.N. & Mitchell, W. (2013). The evolving impact of combinatorial opportunities and exhaustion on innovation by business groups as market development increases: The case of Taiwan. *Management Science*, 59(5), 1142–1161.

Mallin, Ch. 2004. *Corporate governance*. Oxford: Oxford University Press.

Masulis, R., Phan, P. & Zein, J. (2011). Family business groups around the world: Financing advantages, control motivations, and organizational choices. *Review of Financial Studies*, 24(11), 3556–3600.

Meuer, J.R.C. & Backes-Gellner, U. (2015). Layers of co-existing innovation systems. *Research Policy*, 44, 888–910.

Mishra, A. & Akbar, M. (2007). Parenting advantage in business groups of emerging markets. *The Journal of Business Perspective*, 11, 1–10.

Mitra, A. & Pattanayak, M. (2013). Business groups, block holdings and firm value. *International Journal of Disclosure and Governance*, 10(1), 39–57.

Monks, R. & Minow, N. (2004). *Corporate governance*. Malden, MA: Blackwell Business.

Morck, R. & Yeung, B. (2010). Harmonious corporate governance. *Procedia Social and Behavioral Sciences*, 2, 6875–6882.

OECD (2015). G20/OECD principles of corporate governance, https://www.oecd-ilibrary.org/governance/g20-oecd-principles-of-corporate-governance-2015_9789264236882-en (Accessed: 1 September 2021).

Oh, W.J., Chang, Y.K., Lee, G. & Seo, J. (2018). Intragroup transactions, corporate governance, and corporate philanthropy in Korean business groups. *Journal of Business Ethics*, 153, 1031–1049.

Patel, S., Balic, A. & Bwakira, L. (2002). Measuring transparency and disclosure at firm-level in emerging markets. *Emerging Market Review*, 3, 310–324.

Perkins, S., Morck, R. & Young, B. (2014). Innocents abroad: The hazards of international joint ventures with pyramidal group firms. *Global Strategy Journal*, 4, 310–330.

Poczter, S. (2018) Business groups in emerging markets: A survey and analysis. *Emerging Markets Finance and Trade*, 54(5), 1150–1182.

Pursey, P., Heugens, P. & Zyglidopoulos, S. (2008). From social ties to embedded competencies: The case of business groups. *Journal of Management and Governance*, 12, 325–341.

Sanan, N.K., Jaisinghani, D. & Yadav, S. (2019). Corporate governance, firm performance, and business group affiliation: Evidence from India. *Management Decision*, 58(8), 1863–1876.

Schnyder, G. (2012). Varieties of insider corporate governance: The determinants of business preferences and corporate governance reform in the Netherlands, Sweden and Switzerland. *Journal of European Public Policy*, 19(9), 1434–1451.

Selekler-Goksen, N.N. & Öktem, Ö.Y. (2009). Countervailing institutional forces: Corporate governance in Turkish family business groups. *Journal of Management and Governance*, 13, 193–213.

Seran, T., Pellegrin-Boucher, E. & Gurau, C. (2016). The management of coopetitive tensions within multi-unit organizations. *Industrial Marketing Management*, 53, 31–41.

Song, J., Lee, K. & Khanna, T. (2016). Dynamic capabilities at Samsung: Optimizing internal co-opetition. *California Management Review*, 58(4), 118–140.

Stein, J. (1997). Internal capital markets and the competition for corporate resources. *Journal of Finance*, 52, 111–133.

Tidström, A. (2014). Managing tensions in coopetition. *Industrial Marketing Management*, 43, 261–271.

Tidström, A. & Rajala, A. (2016). Coopetition strategy as interrelated praxis and practices on multiple levels. *Industrial Marketing Management*, 58, 35–44.

Tricker, B. (2012). *Corporate governance. Principles, policies and practices*. Oxford: Oxford University Press.

Villalonga, B. (2004). Diversification discount or premium? New evidence from BITS establishment-kevel data. *Journal of Finance*, 59, 479–506.

Yaprak, A. & Karademir, B. (2010). The internationalization of emerging market business groups: An integrated literature review. *International Marketing Review*, 27(2), 245–262.

Yiu, D., Lu, G., Bruton, G. & Hoskisson, R. (2007). Business groups: An integrated model of focus future research. *Journal of Management Studies*, 44, 1555–1570.

Zattoni, A. (1999). The structure of corporate groups: The Italian case. *Corporate Governance*, 7(1), 38–48.

Zattoni, A., & Cuomo, F. (2008) Why adopt codes of good governance? A comparison of institutional and efficiency perspective. *Corporate Governance. An International Review*, 16, 1–15.

8 Coopetition within Business Groups in High-, Medium-, and Low-Tech Industries

Patryk Dziurski

Introduction

Coopetition between standalone entities as well as within business groups emerges in high-, medium-, and low-tech industries. It can be easily traced in high-tech industries, such as electronics (Chen & Chen, 2011), aerospace (Ritala et al., 2017), ICT (Leite et al., 2018), video games (Klimas & Czakon, 2018), and telecommunication (Miri-Lavassani, 2017), but the coopetition strategy is also implemented by entities in medium-tech industries, such as healthcare (van den Broek et al., 2018), automotive (Albort-Morant et al., 2018), and financial services (Mahgoub et al., 2018), as well as low-tech industries, such as textile (Caldeira et al., 2017), organic food (Stanciu et al., 2018), craft beer (Kraus et al., 2019), tourism, and hospitality (Idrees et al., 2018). Therefore, coopetition is a far-reaching phenomenon that occurs across the economy. However, the literature often indicates that the coopetition is pursued more often in high-tech industries (Cygler, 2009b; Wang & Hsu, 2014; Nemeh & Yami, 2019) as high-technology context encourages simultaneous cooperation and competition (Gnyawali & Park, 2011) and makes coopetition relationships more complex (Cygler, 2009a). Moreover, high-tech industries often portray an industry-wide cooperative mindset (Rusko, 2011; Ritala et al., 2014) showing that successful coopetition between some entities in the industry leads to implementation of the coopetition strategy by others therein (Gnyawali & Park, 2011). In this way, coopetition fosters and encourages further coopetition (Crick, 2017) enabling sustainable expansion of an industry (Rusko, 2011). It shows that coopetition is a common and complex strategy in high-tech industries, but it is also pursued by organisations in medium- and low-tech industries as well. It is, therefore, worth to further analyse coopetition in different industrial contexts.

The study sheds light on business groups that operate strategically in multiple markets under common control and ownership (Colpan & Hikino, 2010). Business groups consist of subsidiaries, affiliates, and associated companies (Zattoni, 1999) that simultaneously cooperate and compete (Luo, 2005). Hence, coopetition can be easily traced in business groups (Luo, 2005; Aluchna, 2013; Mierzejewska, 2018, 2022). However, the

DOI: 10.4324/9781003324775-9

literature rarely focuses on intrafirm coopetition within business groups and lacks empirical evidence on types of coopetition in different industrial settings (high-, medium-, and low-tech industries). Some studies point only to external industry-related factors under which coopetition is more likely to occur in business groups, but they are rather scarce (Li et al., 2009; Chambers, 2015; Dorn et al., 2016). Therefore, the chapter aims to identify the prevalent coopetition type implemented by business groups in high-, medium-, and low-tech industries and verify if the technological intensity of an industry impacts type of coopetition within a business group. According to the author's knowledge, this study is the first one to investigate types of coopetition within business groups in Poland with a broad sample of different industries. Identifying various types of coopetition in different industries appears to be fruitful because it allows for more differentiated insights on the importance of different drivers of coopetition within business groups.

Theoretical Lenses

The literature identifies various internal and external drivers of coopetition (Cygler, 2009b; Dorn et al., 2016) indicating that an industry in which an entity operates is an important external factor of coopetition (Gnyawali & Park, 2011; Czakon et al., 2014). The literature also provides different taxonomies of an industry that are very often based on technological intensity and change (Castellacci, 2008; Peneder, 2010). Nevertheless, the most common taxonomy divides industries into high-, medium-, and low-tech. Eurostat, based on simple R&D indicators (R&D expenditure and number of employees with higher education), divides manufacturing industries into high-technology, medium high-technology, medium low-technology, and low-technology (www1), while it also identifies knowledge-intensive services (KIS) and less knowledge-intensive services (LKIS) (www2).

High-tech industries (e.g. manufacture of basic pharmaceutical products and pharmaceutical preparations, telecommunication, advertising and market research, financial service activities, creative, arts, and entertainment) bear certain distinguishing characteristics as compared to less technologically advanced industries (medium- and low-tech industries). High-tech industries are ones characterised by a great innovativeness showing the ability of firms therein to create and implement speedily different types of innovations on a constant basis (Zakrzewska-Bielawska, 2010). Additionally, high level of uncertainty, instability (Padula & Dagnino, 2007; Ritala 2012; Yami & Nemeh, 2014), and technological complexity (Dai, 2008; Oshri & Weeber, 2006; Yami & Nemeh, 2014) increase the level of complexity of products created. Those industries are also characterised by technological convergence, on the one hand (Bengtsson & Raza-Ullah, 2016; Daidj & Egert, 2018), and a growing level of technological specialisation, on the other hand, which is conducive to technological acceleration, shortened product life cycle, increased R&D expenditure (Bouncken et al., 2015), and active approach to the protection of intellectual property. Capital expenditure of firms in high-tech industries is significant as there is the frequent need for upgrading to more innovative technological equipment. High-tech industries, where employees with higher education can find a job easily, operate at the intersection of science and industry converting results of the research into products that are suitable for commercialisation; however, such products tend to age quickly, which then accelerates the drive for innovation (Zakrzewska-Bielawska, 2010).

High-tech industries play an important role in the economy as they are perceived as a key determinant of its innovativeness and competitiveness (Haschka & Herwartz, 2020). High-tech industries create new knowledge, adapt research results to needs of a society, and intensify technological competition between firms that positively impacts on the quality of products. Additionally, growth of high-tech industries translates into the introduction of innovations that often create new needs in a society and enable growth of medium- and low-tech industries (Hirsch-Kreinsen, 2008).

Medium- and low-tech industries (e.g. manufacture of household appliances, metal and plastic products, food, wood, and furniture industries) are characterised by relatively low R&D intensity, and therefore they are named as not research-intensive industries (Hirsch-Kreinsen, 2008). It is assumed that they are less innovative as they have fewer employees dedicated to R&D projects and suppliers are often their main source of knowledge in the innovation process. Moreover, capital expenditure of firms in medium- and low-tech industries is relatively small, and they are a large user of government funding for the purchase of different machinery as well as equipment (de Oliveira Costa et al., 2016). Köhler and Schmierl (1991) point out that low-tech industries produce little scientific knowledge, but they use the process of learning to produce practical knowledge. Learning by doing or learning by using increase and deepen knowledge base in medium- and low-tech industries, which allows firms to innovate and actively respond to market changing conditions. Thus, firms in medium- and low-tech industries innovate, but they focus is often on process innovation (de Oliveira Costa et al., 2016).

Firms and business groups that operate in high-tech industries often face many challenges in innovation and competitiveness. Thus, the literature points to coopetition as being a frequently executed strategy in high-tech industries (Cygler, 2009b; Zakrzewska-Bielawska, 2010; Nemeh & Yami, 2019), which is stimulated by the high technological intensity of an industry (Cygler, 2009a). Features of high-tech industries induce firms and business groups to implement a coopetition strategy (Bouncken et al., 2015) to improve market attractiveness of their products, implement flexible and efficient production processes, and maintain a modern ITC infrastructure, which compels innovation and increased R&D expenditure (Gnyawali & Park, 2011; Bouncken & Fredrich, 2012). Additionally, coopetition in high-tech industries allows entities to grow, provides access to strategic tangible and intangible resources, and enables cost reduction and mitigation of different risks (Bouncken & Kraus, 2013; Le Roy et al., 2021). The coopetition in high-tech industries is, therefore, chosen not only to survive but mainly to thrive.

Coopetition is often implemented by firms and business groups in high-tech industries since it has a positive impact on the number and novelty of innovations created (Gnyawali & Park, 2011; Bouncken et al., 2018; Nemeh & Yami, 2019; Le Roy et al., 2021), even though the literature also points to the possibility of adverse or neutral impact (Ritala, 2012; Liu, 2013; Klimas & Czakon, 2018). The contradictory results are explained, on the one hand, by the impact of external factors, such as environment uncertainty, on the relationship between coopetition and the number of innovations and, on the other hand, internal factors such as absorptive learning capacity, knowledge sharing or formal knowledge protection mechanisms. Another important factor is the type of innovation created as the horizontal coopetition impacts positively the market performance of radical innovation (Le Roy et al., 2021). Entities in high-tech industries face significant pressure to innovate and open innovation process ever more broadly, which compels the constant improvement of innovativeness and is conducive to intra- and inter-organisational relationships, also with competitors. Thus, coopetition is a driver of innovation and, thereby, success. It is, however, worth noting that the innovativeness of an entity is an important driver of coopetition too (Klimas & Czakon, 2018). It means that an entity's innovativeness is an important determinant of coopetition, which, as a result, allows the firm or business group's innovativeness to be improved.

It is indicated that belonging to a high-tech industry is an important determinant of coopetition. Thus, it means that business groups operating in high-tech industries show a greater propensity to coopetition within a business group than ones operating in medium- and low-tech industries. On the one hand, technological pressure and intensity of high-tech industries incentivise cooperation within business groups due to relationships already present among subsidiaries, relative ease of establishing and maintaining such relationships, ability to amplify benefits of cooperation (Kumar & Dutta, 2017), and reduction of different risks intrinsic to intra- and inter-organisational cooperation. On the other hand, the technological advancement of high-tech industries may have an adverse impact on cooperation among subsidiaries due to the lack of suitable tangible and intangible resources within an entity or incompatibility of technologies or goals (Song et al., 2016) prompting subsidiaries to look for partners outside of the business group and reduce internal cooperation. However, internal cooperation within a business group is the first option for subsidiaries, hence, operating in high-tech industries is a catalyst for cooperation within a business group, but simultaneously it does not translate into low-intensity competition. High-tech industries require significant R&D expenditure and high flexibility and efficiency in innovation processes that intensify competition among subsidiaries for the parent company's resources and support, position in the business group, and market expansion (Luo, 2005).

The technological advancement of high-tech industries affects not only the intensity of cooperation and competition (Klimas & Czakon, 2018; Ritala, 2021) but also the complexity of coopetitive relationships within business groups (Cygler, 2009a). A study on the wireless telecommunication industry in Europe, that is accounted to high-tech industries, shows that multiple coopetition (with more than two partners) is conducive to radical innovation (Nemeh & Yami, 2019), which, in turn, is key to survival and success in innovative industries. To survive and thrive, business groups operating in high-tech industries pursue complex network coopetition that involves multiple partners within the business group and large number of value chain areas. The aim of complex network coopetition is to response actively to the high technological intensity of an industry, increase flexibility, and create and implement innovations enabling the enhancement of competitiveness.

To sum up, coopetition is common strategy in high-tech industries; however, it is also pursed by entities in medium- and low-tech industries. Nevertheless, the literature indicates that the coopetition in high-tech industries differs compared to one in medium and low-tech industries. Coopetition within business groups operating in high-tech industries is characterised by high-intensity cooperation and competition, while in medium- and low-tech industries, it exhibits low-intensity cooperation and competition or even no coopetition at all. When it comes to complexity, business groups in high-tech industries adopt more often complex network coopetition, whereas business groups from medium- and low-tech industries pursue simple unidirectional coopetition.

Empirical Findings

The study, which results are presented in the chapter, uses a survey database of 121 business groups in Poland that was drawn from the databases of business groups that a parent company is listed on the Warsaw Stock Exchange. Data were acquired from surveys with top managers of parent companies from randomly selected business groups, Amadeus database and financial statements published by business groups. Information about the research sample and method is presented in the introduction, while measures of coopetition and coopetition models are elaborated in Chapter 2.

The literature review shows that the coopetition among standalone entities in industries of varied technological advancement (high-, medium-, and low-tech) is a frequent subject of many studies; however, the number of research focusing on business groups is not sufficient. Thus, it is important to identify the prevalent coopetition type implemented by business groups operating in high-, medium-, and low-tech industries and verify if the technological intensity of an industry impacts type of coopetition within a business group.

The study uses Eurostat's industry taxonomy. Eurostat's high-tech statistics on high-tech industry and KIS includes economics, employment and science, technology, and innovation (STI) data that describes manufacturing and service industries/products based on technological intensity. Eurostat created the industry taxonomy using two approaches to identify technological intensity of an industry: sectoral and product. The sectoral approach utilises R&D expenditures/value added for manufacturing industries to NACE at 2-digit level (NACE is a statistical classification of economic activities in the European Community), while services industries are divided into KIS and LKIS based on the share of tertiary educated persons to NACE at 2-digit level. Eurostat also created the knowledge intensive activities approach (KIA), which is a single methodology for manufacturing and service industries as well as for public sector activities. It is based on the share of educated people in each industry to NACE at 2-digit level. The sectoral approach is complemented by the product approach that uses data on high-tech trade. The list of high-technology products is based on the calculation of R&D intensity (R&D expenditure/total sales) by groups of products and aggregated based on the Standard International Trade Classification (SITC) (www3).

Business groups are accounted to high-, medium-, and low-tech industry based on analysis of their respective main area of operations in line with NACE 2-digit level following the Eurostat's industry taxonomy (www1; www2). Information about the main area of operation of business groups sampled was collected from the Amadeus database. The study distinguishes high-tech industries (high-technology manufacturing industries and KIS), medium-tech industries (medium high-technology and medium low-technology manufacturing industries, as well as LKIS), and low-tech industries (low-technology manufacturing industries and other services not classified as a KIS or LKIS). Table 8.1 shows the number of business groups in high-, medium-, and low-tech industries in the sample.

Table 8.1 Business groups in high-, medium-, and low-tech industries

Industry	*Frequencies*	*Percentage*	*Cumulative percentage*
High-tech industries	32	26.4	26.4
Medium-tech industries	53	43.8	70.2
Low-tech industries	36	29.8	100

Source: Own elaboration.

The research sample is diversified as 43.8% of business groups have their main area of operations in medium-tech industries, whereas 29.8% of the sample operate in low-tech industries and 26.4% in high-tech industries.

The literature review shows that the technological intensity of an industry in which a business group operates in triggers simultaneous cooperation and competition. Coopetition within a business group can be characterised by the direction of coopetition (see Chapter 2). The study identifies two main coopetition types implemented by business groups studied: (1) network (112 business groups) and (2) unidirectional coopetition (9 business groups). Therefore, the study makes it possible to identify the prevalent coopetition type implemented by business groups in high-, medium-, and low-tech industries and determine whether business groups in industries of different technological intensity adopt network or unidirectional coopetition. However, the technological intensity of an industry in which a business group operates in does not differentiate them. Putting it differently, business groups, regardless the technological intensity of an industry, implement mainly network coopetition. The chi-squared test also does not confirm the existence of statistically significant differences among business groups studied regarding coopetition type and the technological intensity of an industry ($p = 0.947$). Thus, the literature-based assumption that business groups in high-tech industries tend to choose more network and complex coopetition, while business groups in medium- and low-tech industries implement more unidirectional and simple coopetition cannot be confirmed.

Coopetition within a business group can be also characterised by the intensity of competition and cooperation. In the study, four- and nine-field matrix of coopetition are used (see Chapter 2). In the four-field matrix, the intensity of cooperation and competition is divided into low and high, while in the nine-field matrix is split into low, medium, and high. Therefore, the study makes it possible to determine the prevalent coopetition type implemented by business groups in high-, medium-, and low-tech industries and answer the question if the technological intensity of an industry impacts type of coopetition within a business group.

The study applies four-field matrix of coopetition and identifies two main types of coopetition: (1) low cooperation and competition (15 business groups), and (2) high cooperation and low competition (106 business groups). However, the technological intensity of an industry in which a business group operates in does not differentiate them. In other words, business groups, regardless the technological intensity of an industry, pursue coopetition type with high cooperation and low competition. Moreover, the chi-squared test does not confirm the existence of statistically significant differences among business groups studied regarding coopetition type identified based on four-field coopetition matrix and the technological intensity of an industry ($p = 0.957$).

Table 8.2 Coopetition types based on nine-field coopetition matrix versus the technological intensity of an industry in which business groups studied operate in

Industry	*Coopetition type*					*Total*
	Low cooperation and competition	*Medium cooperation and low competition*	*Medium cooperation and competition*	*High cooperation and low competition*	*High cooperation and medium competition*	
High-tech industries	0 (0%)	1 (3.1%)	3 (9.4%)	18 (56.3%)	10 (31.2%)	100%
Medium-tech industries	1 (1.9%)	6 (11.3%)	0 (0%)	34 (64.2%)	12 (22.6%)	100%
Low-tech industries	0 (0%)	3 (8.3%)	1 (2.8%)	26 (72.2%)	6 (16.7%)	100%

Source: Own elaboration.
$p = 0.416$; $\chi^2 = 6{,}569$.

The study also uses nine-field coopetition matrix. Table 8.2 presents results of the chi-squared test on relationship between coopetition types based on nine-field coopetition matrix within business groups and the technological intensity of an industry in which they operate in.

The study allows to identify five types of coopetition within business groups studied based on the nine-field matrix: (1) high cooperation and low competition (78 business groups), (2) high cooperation and medium competition (28 business groups), (3) medium cooperation and low competition (10 business groups), (4) medium cooperation and competition (4 business groups), and (5) low cooperation and competition (1 business group). However, the chi-squared test does not confirm the existence of statistically significant differences among business groups studied regarding coopetition types based on nine-field coopetition matrix and the technological intensity of an industry. However, some conclusions might be drawn. The analysis conducted shows that the most frequently implemented coopetition type is the one characterised by high cooperation and low competition irrespective to the technological intensity of an industry of business groups sampled. It must be noted, however, that this type is more prevalent in low- and medium-tech industries than high-tech industries. Moreover, business groups in high-tech industries pursue more often coopetition type with a high cooperation and medium competition than business groups in medium- and low-tech industries. Those in high-tech industries may experience relatively higher internal and external competitive pressure that could be caused by high technological advancement of an industry, hence, might be more likely to choose coopetition type characterised by high cooperation and medium competition. However,

Table 8.3 Competition intensity versus the technological intensity of an industry in which business groups studied operate in

Industry	*Competition intensity within a business group*		
	Very low	*Low*	*Medium*
High-tech industry	9 (28.1%)	10 (31.3%)	13 (40.6%)
Medium-tech industry	30 (56.6%)	11 (20.8%)	12 (22.6%)
Low-tech industry	12 (33.3%)	17 (47.2%)	7 (19.5%)

Source: Own study.
$p = 0.011$; $\chi^2 = 0{,}319$.

this is not confirmed by the chi-squared test, thus the literature-based assumption that business groups in high-tech industries tend to implement coopetition type characterised by high-intensity cooperation and competition, while business groups in medium- and low-tech industries pursue one characterised by low-intensity cooperation and competition cannot be confirmed.

The analysis conducted shows that business groups in medium- and high-tech industries choose relatively more frequently coopetition type with more intense competition; therefore, additional analysis was conducted. It is examined if there is a relationship between competition intensity within business groups and the technological intensity of an industry. The result of the analysis conducted is presented in Table 8.3.

The chi-squared test confirms the existence of statistically significant differences among business groups studied regarding the technological intensity of an industry in which business groups studied operate in. It means that business groups in high-tech industries experience higher competition intensity (it was indicated by respondents as medium more often than as very low or low) than business groups in medium- and low-tech industries (it was indicated by respondents as very low or low more often than as medium). The result, therefore, confirms the literature-based assumption that business groups in high-tech industries are characterised by a higher level of competition intensity compared to business groups in medium- and low-tech industries. Thus, the technological intensity of an industry impacts competition intensity within a business group.

Conclusion

The chapter aims to identify the prevalent coopetition type implemented by business groups studied in high-, medium-, and low-tech industries and answer the question whether the industry (high-, medium-, and low-tech) leads to different choices of coopetition types among business groups. First, the literature that focuses mainly on coopetition among standalone entities indicates that entities in high-tech industries implement more frequently coopetition than organisations in medium- and low-tech industries. Second, coopetition in high-tech industries could be characterised by higher intensity of cooperation, competition, complexity, and networking compared to coopetition pursed by entities in medium- and low-tech industries. The literature identifies the increasing R&D expenditure, shortening life cycles of products, and technological convergence as the main external drivers of coopetition (Gnyawali & Park, 2011). Those characteristics are attributed to high-tech industries (Zakrzewska-Bielawska, 2010) and thus entities of those industries implement coopetition more frequently than ones in medium- and low-tech industries (Cygler, 2009b; Wang & Hsu, 2014; Nemeh & Yami, 2019), while the coopetition itself is characterised by high level of networking and complexity (Cygler, 2009a). The study, however, does not find support for such conclusions since no statistically significant differences are found to exist in coopetition types followed by business groups from high-, medium-, and low-tech industries in Poland. The study confirms only that there are differences in competition intensity between business groups in high-, medium-, and low-tech industries (business groups in high-tech industries experience more intense competition than business groups in medium- and low-tech industries), but it does not constitute a differentiating factor in coopetition types.

The results of the study do not confirm literature-based assumptions on the relationship between technological intensity of an industry and type of coopetition within a business group. However, business groups are complex organisations that significantly differs from standalone firms, and therefore, conclusions from studies into coopetition among standalone entities might not apply to business groups. Business groups are created because market institutions are inefficient (Cainelli & Iacobucci, 2011; Holmes et al., 2015) and there is the desire to benefit from cooperation among different entities (Powell & Smith-Doerr, 1994); however, they evolve and adopt to the changing environment along the economic growth and development (Colpan & Cuervo-Cazurra, 2018). Business groups are thus an important agent of the economic system both in developing and developed economies (Holmes et al., 2015; Colpan & Cuervo-Cazurra, 2018). Cooperation within a business group is a natural relationship that occurs among subsidiaries irrespective of the industry in which they operate. In other words, cooperation within a business group is not a response to the growing technological intensity of an industry, but a relationship inextricably linked to the realisation of benefits by all members of a business group. Moreover, business groups are complex organisations (Holmes et al., 2015) that choose to implement coopetition for many different internal and external reasons (see Chapter 4) and the technological intensity of an industry may not be the factor of the highest significant to differentiate business groups' implemented coopetition type. Therefore, different factors might be more important to encourage and compel the simultaneous cooperation and competition within a business group.

References

Albort-Morant, G., Leal-Millan, A., Cepeda-Carrion, G. & Henseler, J. (2018). Developing green innovation performance by fostering of organizational knowledge and coopetitive relations. *Review of Managerial Science*, 12(2), 499–517.

Bengtsson, M. & Raza-Ullah, T. (2016). A systematic review of research on coopetition: Toward a multilevel understanding. *Industrial Marketing Management*, 57, 23–39.

Bouncken, R. & Fredrich, V. (2012). Coopetition: Performance implications and management antecedents. *International Journal of Innovation Management*, 16(5), 1250028.

Bouncken, R.B., Fredrich, V., Ritala, P. & Kraus, S. (2018). Coopetition in new product development alliances: Advantages and tensions for incremental and radical Innovation. *British Journal of Management*, 29(3), 391–410.

Bouncken, R.B., Gast, J., Kraus, S. & Bogers, M. (2015). Coopetition: A systematic review, synthesis, and future research directions. *Review of Management Science*, 9, 577–601.

Bouncken, R.B. & Kraus, S. (2013). Innovation in knowledge-intensive industries: The double-edged sword of coopetition. *Journal of Business Research*, 66(10), 2060–2070.

Cainelli, G. & Iacobucci, D. (2011). Business groups and the boundaries of the firm. *Management Decision*, 49(9), 1549–1573.

Caldeira, A., de Fátima Fonseca, A., Gonzales, D.A. & de Souza, K.G. (2017). Cooperative strategies for competitiveness in the Brazilian textile sector: The role of class entities. *Sistemas & Gestao*, 12(2), 295–307.

Castellacci, F. (2008). Technological paradigms, regimes and trajectories: Manufacturing and service industries in a new taxonomy of sectoral patterns of innovation. *Research Policy*, 39(6–7), 978–994.

Chambers, M. (2015). *Dynamic inter-subsidiary relationships of competition and collaboration*. Dissertation. Cranfield University.

Chen, Y-S. & Chen, B-Y. (2011). Utilizing patent analysis to explore the cooperative competition relationship of the two LED companies: Nichia and Osram. *Technological Forecasting and Social Change*, 78(2), 294–302.

Colpan, A.M. & Cuervo-Cazurra, A. (2018). *Business groups as an organizational model*, in *Oxford research encyclopedia of business and management*. Oxford: Oxford University Press.

Colpan, A.M. & Hikino, T. (2010). *Foundations of business groups: Towards an integrated framework*, in Colpan, A.M., Hikino, & Lincoln, J.R. (eds.) *The Oxford handbook of business groups*. Oxford: Oxford University Press, 15–66.

Crick, J.M. (2017). The facets, antecedents and consequences of coopetition: An entrepreneurial marketing perspective. *Qualitative Market Research*, 21(2), 253–272.

Cygler, J. (2009a). *Kooperencja przedsiębiorstw. Czynniki sektorowe i korporacyjne [Firms coopetition. Industry-related and corporate factors]*. Warszawa: Oficyn Wydawnicza SGH.

Cygler, J. (2009b). Sectoral and corporate coopetitive factors – coopetition matrix. *Journal of Management and Financial Sciences*, 2(2), 77–96.

Czakon, W. Mucha-Kuś, K. & Rogalski, M. (2014). Coopetition research landscape – A systematic literature review 1997–2010. *Journal of Economics & Management*, 17, 122–150.

Dai, L. (2008). Maximizing cooperation in a competitive environment. *Competition Forum*, 6(1), 63–74.

Daidj, N. & Egert, Ch. (2018). Towards new coopetition-based business models? The case of Netflix on the French market. *Journal of Research in Marketing and Entrepreneurship*, 20(1), 99–120.

de Oliveira Costa, E., Cabral, J.E.O., Forte, S.H.A.C., & Costa, M.D.P.B. (2016). Patterns of technological innovation: A comparative analysis between low-tech and high-tech industries in Brazil. *International Journal of Innovation*, 4(2), 97–105.

Dorn, S., Schweiger, B. & Albers, S. (2016). Levels, phases and themes of coopetition: A systematic literature review and research agenda. *European Management Journal*, 34(5), 484–500.

Gnyawali, D.R. & Park, B-J. (2011). Co-opetition between giants: Collaboration with competitors for technological innovation. *Research Policy*, 40(5), 650–663.

Haschka, R.E. & Herwartz, H. (2020). Innovation efficiency in European high-tech industries: Evidence from a Bayesian stochastic frontier approach. *Research Policy*, 49(8), 104054.

Hirsch-Kreinsen, H. (2008). "Low-technology": A forgotten sector in innovation policy. *Journal of Technology Management & Innovation*, 3(3), 11–20.

Holmes, R.M., Hoskisson, R.E., Kim, H., Wan, W.P. & Holcomb, T.R. (2015). International strategy and business groups: A review and future research agenda. *Journal of World Business*, 53(2), 134–150.

Idrees, I.A., Vasconcelos, A.C. & Ellis, D. (2018). Clique and elite: Inter-organizational knowledge sharing across five star hotels in the Saudi Arabian religious tourism and hospitality industry. *Journal of Knowledge Management*, 22(-6), 1358–1378.

Klimas, P. & Czakon, W. (2018). Organizational innovativeness and coopetition: A study of video game developers. *Review of Managerial Science*, 12(2), 379–383.

Köhler, C. & Schmierl, K. (1991). Diffusion of cim-technologies and trends in work organization. *Structural Change and Economic Dynamics*, 2(2), 381–394.

Kraus, S., Klimas, P., Gast, J. & Stephan, T. (2019). Sleeping with competitors: Forms, antecedents and outcomes of coopetition of small and medium-sized craft beer breweries. *International Journal of Entrepreneurial Behavior & Research*, 25(1), 50–66.

Kumar, A. & Dutta, S.K. (2017). Tacit knowledge transfer in coopetition: An empirical investigation of the role of business group (BG) affiliation. *Journal of Strategy and Management*, 10(4), 453–468.

Leite, E., Pahlberg, C. & Åberg, S. (2018). The cooperation-competition interplay in the ICT industry. *Journal of Business & Industrial Marketing*, 33(4), 495–505.

Le Roy, F., Robert, F. & Hamouti, R. (2021). Vertical vs horizontal coopetition and the market performance of product innovation: An empirical study of the video game industry. *Technovation*, 112, 102411

Li, D., Ferreira, M. P., & Serra, F. R. (2009). Technology transfer within MNEs: Inter-subsidiary competition and cooperation. *RAI-Revista de Administração e Inovação, 6*(1), 139–158.

Liu, R. (2013). Cooperation, competition and coopetition in innovation communities. *Prometheus,* 13(2), 91–105.

Luo, Y. (2005). Toward coopetition within a multinational enterprise: A perspective from foreign subsidiaries. *Journal of World Business,* 40(1), 71–90.

Mahgoub, Y., Arvidsson, N. & Urueña, A. (2018). Emergence of a digital platform based disruptive mobile payments service. *International Journal of E-Business Research,* 14(3), 1–19.

Mierzejewska, W. (2018). Koopetycja w grupach kapitałowych [Coopetition in business groups]. *Studia Ekonomiczne,* 351, 121–130.

Mierzejewska, W. (2022). Understanding coopetition within multinational corporations: the perspective of relationship between subsidiaries. *Global Journal of Flexible Systems Management,* 23, 371–385.

Miri-Lavassani, K. (2017). Coopetition and sustainable competitiveness in business ecosystem: A networks analysis of the global telecommunications industry. *Transnational Corporations Review,* 9(4), 281–308.

Nemeh, A. & Yami, S. (2019). Orchestrating resources for FMA in coopetitive NPD. *R&D Management,* 49(1), 64–85.

Oshri, I. & Weeber, C. (2006). Cooperation and competition standards-setting activities in the digitization era: The case of wireless information devices. *Technology Analysis & Strategic Management,* 18(2), 265–283.

Padula, G. & Dagnino, G.B. (2007). Untangling the rise of coopetition. *International Studies of Management and Organization,* 37(2), 32–52.

Peneder, M. (2010). Technological regimes and the variety of innovation behaviour: Creating integrated taxonomies of firms and sectors. *Research Policy,* 39(3), 323–334.

Powell, W.W. & Smith-Doerr, L. (1994). *Networks and economic life,* in Smelser, N.J. & Swedberg, R. (eds.) *The handbook of economic sociology.* Princeton, NJ: Princeton University Press, 379–402.

Ritala, P. (2012). Coopetition strategy – when is it successful? Empirical evidence on innovation and market performance. *British Journal of Management,* 23(3), 307–324.

Ritala, P., Golnam, A. & Wegmann, A. (2014). Coopetition-based business models: The case of Amazon.com. *Industrial Marketing Management,* 43(2), 236–249.

Ritala, P., Huizingh, E. & Almpanopoulou, A. (2017). Tensions in R&D networks: Implications for knowledge search and integration. *Technological Forecasting and Social Change,* 120, 311–322.

Rusko, R. (2011). Exploring the concept of coopetition: A typology for the strategic moves of the Finnish forest industry. *Industrial Marketing Management,* 40(-2), 311–320.

Song, J., Lee, K. & Khanna, T. (2016). Dynamic capabilities at Samsung: Optimizing internal co-ppetition. *California Management Review,* 58(4), 118–140.

Stanciu, S. Bichescu, C., Căpățînă, A., Dragan, G.B. & Florea, A-M. (2018). Enablers and inhibitors of collaborative network development in organic food industry: A fuzzy set qualitative comparative analysis (fsQCA). *Contemporary Economics,* 12(4), 433–445.

van den Broek, J., Boselie, P. & Paauwe, J. (2018). Cooperative innovation through a talent management pool: A qualitative study on coopetition in healthcare. *European Management Journal*, 36(1), 135–144.

Wang, C.-H. & Hsu, L.-C. (2014). Building exploration and exploration in the high-tech industries: The role of relationship learning. *Technological Forecasting and Social Change*, 81, 331–340.

www1, https://ec.europa.eu/eurostat/statistics-explained/index.php?title=Glossary:High-tech_classification_of_manufacturing_industries (Accessed: 3 June 2022).

www2, https://ec.europa.eu/eurostat/statistics-explained/index.php?title=Glossary:Knowledge-intensive_services_(KIS) (Accessed: 3 June 2022).

www3, https://ec.europa.eu/eurostat/cache/metadata/en/htec_esms.htm (Accessed: 3 June 2022).

Yami, S. & Nemeh, A. (2014). Organizing coopetition for innovation: The case of wireless telecommunication sector in Europe. *Industrial Marketing Management*, 43(2), 250–260.

Zakrzewska-Bielawska, A. (2010). *High technology company – Concept, nature, characteristics*, in Recent Advances in Management, Marketing, Finances: Proceedings of the 8th International Conference on Management, Marketing and Finances (MMF '10), Panang, Malaysia, March 23–25, 2010.

Zattoni, A. (1999). The structure of business groups: The Italian case. *Corporate Governance: An International Review*, 7(1), 38–48.

9 Financial Outcomes of Coopetition within Business Groups

Agnieszka Sopińska

Introduction

The literature clearly shows that the relationship between coopetition strategy and financial performance of an entity is understudied (Bengtsson & Raza-Ullah, 2016; Gernsheimer et al., 2021). Additionally, existing studies mainly focus on the impact of inter-organisational coopetition on financial performance, rather than on intra-organisational coopetition, especially in the context of business groups. It can be concluded that the impact of intra-organisational coopetition on financial performance is mostly uncharted territory. Previous studies focus mostly on influence of the intra-firm coopetition on firm performance concerning knowledge sharing, improved customer orientation, and enhanced ability to innovate (Dorn et al., 2016).

The aim of the chapter is to explore the impact of coopetition in business groups on their financial performance. First, results of studies that focus on the impact of coopetition on financial performance are discussed, and then results of the study on intra-organisational coopetition and its relationship with financial performance are provided. The chapter discusses results of the study carried out on business groups listed on the Warsaw Stock Exchange. The study uses different types of coopetition based on the intensity of competition and cooperation, and the direction of coopetition. The impact of the implemented type of coopetition on financial performance is described through the lens of six financial indicators.

Theoretical Lenses

The relationship between coopetition and financial performance is still not well examined as different studies show mixed results. Additionally, scarce publications in this area focus mostly on inter-organisational, but not on intra-organisational coopetition, especially in the context of complex organisations such as business groups.

A positive impact of coopetition on financial performance is shown by Peng et al. (2012), who analysed 31 financial indicators over 15 years of Taiwanese supermarket chain. The results enable authors to formulate two

DOI: 10.4324/9781003324775-10

conclusions. First, competition (yang) and cooperation (yin) are mutually rooted and promoted. Second, cooperation with competitors improves financial performance, at least for a certain time, due to increased efficiency of each entity involved.

A strong correlation between coopetition and financial performance is also identified by Morris et al. (2007). They studied 647 small businesses in Turkey. The results of the study enable to conclude that coopetition pursued by small businesses in Turkey has a strong positive impact on their financial performance as it allows for a risk mitigation and better utilisation of resources.

The impact of cooperation in innovation with competitors and non-competitors on the financial performance is also the focus of the study undertaken by Pekovic et al. (2020). Authors used the sample of 2,957 French companies that cooperate with competitors and non-competitors. In both cases, cooperation in innovation positively contributes to EBITDA; however, the effect is stronger when cooperation is pursued with non-competitors than competitors. It allows to conclude that benefiting fully from cooperation in innovation with competitors and non-competitors is not automatic, but it requires precise management.

Financial performance is closely linked to operational efficiency as the latter one positively impacts the former one; therefore the relationship between coopetition and operational efficiency should be examined too. Le Roy and Sanou (2014) analyse the mobile telecommunication industry and identify three types of strategies pursued by companies therein: aggressive, cooperative, and coopetitive. The results show that the best efficiency is linked with the coopetitive strategy. Additionally, out of the remaining two strategies, the aggressive strategy is more successful than the cooperative strategy. Thus, it can be concluded that in the context of all three strategies, the coopetitive strategy, by ensuring the best efficiency, improves financial performance. However, Sanou et al. (2016), based on the mobile telecommunication industry, show that the efficiency is dependent on the company's position in the coopetitive network as better position in the network allows to gain better performance. Authors pointed out that a central position in the coopetitive network is advantageous to the firm.

Some studies refer to specific organisations like sport clubs. Robert et al.'s (2009) analyse coopetitive relationships between French soccer teams competing in Ligue 1 and Ligue 2 in the 2005–2006 season. Authors indicate that coopetition among French soccer teams does not improve their sport performance, but it improves their financial performance. Similar conclusions are drawn by Wemmer et al. (2016). Authors studied the impact of coopetition on the financial stability of German sports clubs based on a survey of 292 members of boards of directors of non-commercial sports clubs in the Saarland. The study shows that sports clubs pursuing a coopetition strategy achieve higher levels of financial stability. However, important moderating factors are access to external knowledge and implementation of innovation.

Crick and Crick (2020) show a positive impact of coopetition on sales results of 151 sports clubs from New Zealand. Authors also identify different factors that impact the analysed relationship. Conflicts between sport clubs inhibit positive impact of coopetition on sales performance, while the intensity of competition is a catalysing factor. Therefore, managers should be incentivised to coopetition, especially underfinanced organisations as cooperating with competitors is a strategy that boots sales performance. However, managers should consider the risk of opportunistic behaviours that detriments results. The study of Crick and Crick (2020) also concludes on the impact of the structure of an industry on the success of coopetition. Authors point out that organisations operating in industries with a higher number of competitors have advantage over entities from industries with limited number of competitors as in the first case the number of potential trustworthy partners with complementary resources is greater than in the second case.

Liu et al. (2014) examine the impact of the intensity of coopetition on financial performance. They studied 225 supplier-buyer dyads from the Chinese household appliances industry. The results show that high-competition and high-cooperation coopetition relationships led to better financial performance than low-cooperation and low-competition coopetition relationships.

The impact of coopetition on financial performance is also analysed based on single case studies. Dubois and Fredriksson (2008) analyse the Volvo's triadic relationship with two suppliers and show that coopetition leads to increased effectiveness. Park and Kim (2020) also note improved financial performance because of the cooperation with competitors. Authors use the case study method to show the coopetition between Apple and Samsung in the smartphone industry. Both firms managed to improve their financial performance despite the growing competition in the industry.

In studies discussed, coopetition has a positive impact on operational and financial performance. However, some authors highlight the need to consider other factors to report the linear relationship between coopetition and financial performance. Ritala (2012), based on the cross-industry study of 209 Finnish companies, shows that the coopetition is more suitable in industries characterised by a significant market uncertainty, network operation, and intense competition than in stable industries without intense competition and with low networking as in the second case, the coopetition does not generate a positive impact on the financial performance.

Crick (2019) indicates the lack of linear correlation between coopetition and financial performance. The study, based on data from 101 vineyards in New Zealand, shows that the coopetition has non-linear (squared) relationship with customer-satisfaction, market, and financial results. Author points out that the coopetition is an opportunity and provides firms with new resource, but it also has dark sides. Too low coopetition means that firms may struggle to survive as they do not have a lot of opportunities and sufficient resources, while too high coopetition means increased tensions, potential loss of the intellectual property, and reduced competitive advantage. It must, however, be highlighted that in this study financial performance was only one of three dependent variables considered, which may partially distort conclusions.

Coopetition may be pursed not only at inter-organisational but also at intra-organisational level. The study conducted by Bendig et al. (2018) assesses the relationship between cross-functional coopetition and the company's performance (a synthetic variable), including financial and market performance. The study, based on survey on 331 German companies from different industries, enables to conclude that the cross-functional coopetition has a positive impact on a company's performance, including financial performance. Researchers also find that the organisational learning capacity, which is possible thanks to delegation of authority within an organisation, is the intermediate variable in the relationship studied.

Improvement of the financial and market performance because of the intra-organisational coopetition is also noted by Luo et al. (2006), who collected date from 326 middle managers from 163 corporations. Authors also emphasise the role of organisational learning as the intermediate variable in the relationship between intra-organisational coopetition and financial performance.

Liu et al. (2019), who assess multinational corporations' subsidiaries that sell similar and diverse products, provided different conclusions. Researchers point out that intra-organisational coopetition within a network of subsidiaries that sell similar products has curvilinear impact on the financial performance of foreign subsidiaries (inverted U-shape), whereas a network of subsidiaries that sell diverse products exhibits monotonic (positive) impact.

The research review indicates the potential positive impact of coopetition on firms' financial performance. Most of the research proves financial benefits that may arise because of entering coopetitive relationships. This mainly concerns inter-organisational coopetition research although the positive influence of coopetition on financial results is also noticed at the intra-organisational level. Those are cautious conclusions, and the overview provided in the chapter does not permit clear inferences to be drawn concerning the impact of coopetition on financial performance for several reasons. First, only in few studies, the correlation between coopetition and financial performance constitutes the main area of the research. In many studies, financial performance is considered together with other effects of coopetition. Second, financial performance variables are measured with different indicators, thus rendering comparisons difficult. Third, the basis for inferences previously drawn is provided not only by representative quantitative surveys but also by case studies of organisations pursuing coopetition. Fourth, prior research, mostly, examines inter-organisational and not intra-organisational coopetition. The current state of knowledge of the impact of intra-organisational coopetition on financial performance is by far insufficient and calls for more in-depth studies.

Empirical Findings

The study, which results are presented in the chapter, uses a survey database of 121 business groups in Poland that was drawn from the databases of business groups that a parent company is listed on the Warsaw Stock Exchange. Data were acquired from surveys with top managers of parent companies from randomly selected business groups, Amadeus database and financial statements published by business groups. Information about the research sample and method is presented in the introduction, while measures of coopetition and coopetition types are elaborated in Chapter 2.

This study aims to explore the impact of coopetition in business groups on their financial performance. Financial performance is measured by the following indicators: gross profit [EUR], EBIT margin [%], book value per share [EUR], operating revenue (turnover) [EUR], net income (P/L) [EUR], and total assets [EUR]. Descriptive statistics of analysed financial indicators are provided in Table 9.1.

Results show that financial performance of business groups studied is highly heterogeneous. The average values for each of financial indicators were above zero, but there still exists high differentials between minimum and maximum values for the sample.

Table 9.1 Descriptive statistics for financial indicators of business groups analysed

Financial indicators	*N*[a]	*Minimum*	*Maximum*	*Average*	*Standard deviation*
Gross profit [EUR]	91	−72,505.00	1,042,450.00	63,098.44	174,060.84
EBIT Margin [%]	111	−90.00	69.00	2.65	18.48
Book value per share [EUR]	111	−5.00	108.00	6.14	13.25
Operating revenue [EUR]	113	36.00	9,578,479.00	477,092.71	1,267,803.67
Net income [EUR]	113	−107,709.00	745,437.00	20,927.52	91,105.92
Total assets [EUR]	113	24.00	14,899,676.00	788,638.90	2,341,369.34

Source: Own elaboration.

a Different N for each financial indicator due to no access to data.

The analysis of descriptive statistics of financial indicators of business groups analysed is a starting point for further analysis into the impact of intra-organisational coopetition within business groups on their financial performance. Author intents to check whether the type of intra-organisational coopetition affects financial performance of business groups in the sample, and if so, then whether it is possible to identify which type of coopetition improves financial performance.

Intra-organisational coopetition can be considered from different perspectives that allow to identify different types of such coopetition. The study uses two criteria: intensity of competition and cooperation, and the direction of coopetition to assess the impact of coopetition on financial performance.

Cooperation and competition intensities are gradable and thus they can be measured on a scale. In the study, four- and nine-field matrix of coopetition types are used (see Chapter 2). In the four-field matrix, the intensity of cooperation and competition is divided into low and high, while in the nine-field matrix is split into low, medium, and high.

Nine-field matrix allows to identify five types of coopetition in business groups studied: (1) high cooperation and low competition (78 business groups), (2) high cooperation and medium competition (28 business groups), (3) medium cooperation and low competition (10 business groups), (4) medium cooperation and competition (4 business groups), and (5) low cooperation and competition (1 business group). The Kruskal-Wallis' test does not confirm the existence of statistically significant differences among business groups studied regarding coopetition types and financial performance. Asymptotic significance is higher than 0.05.

The inability to formulate conclusions, concerning the impact of the type of coopetition distinguished based on the nine-field matrix on financial performance of business groups studied, promotes the use of four-field matrix that allows to identify two types of coopetition: (1) low cooperation and competition (15 business groups), and (2) high cooperation and low competition (106 business groups). Table 9.2 provides average values of financial indicators analysed for both types of competition distinguished based on cooperation and competition intensities.

The results of the study on relationship between coopetition type and financial performance are not unequivocal. Business groups pursuing a high cooperation and low competition exhibit higher average values of four out of six financial indicators analysed, namely, operating revenue, net income, total assets, and gross profit, while business groups following a low cooperation and competition score better on two indicators: EBIT margin and book value per share. Unfortunately, the viability of drawing further conclusions is limited because the Mann-Whitney U test does not confirm the existence of statistically significant differences between groups distinguished according to the above two coopetition types. Asymptotic significance is higher than 0.05.

Table 9.2 Coopetition types based on four-field coopetition matrix versus financial performance of business groups studied

Financial indicators	*Low cooperation and competition*		*High cooperation and low competition*	
	N[a]	*Average*	*N*[a]	*Average*
Gross profit [EUR]	9	32,847.92	82	66,418.62
EBIT Margin [%]	12	4.57	99	2.42
Book value per share [EUR]	12	9.90	99	5.69
Operating revenue [EUR]	12	280,382.00	101	500,464.28
Net Income [EUR]	12	11,204.32	101	22,082.75
Total assets [EUR]	12	306,101.97	101	845,970.02

Source: Own elaboration.
a Different N for each financial indicator due to no access to data.

In summary, no statistically significant correlation is found between type of coopetition distinguished based on the cooperation and competition intensities and financial performance of business groups studied. Neither is it possible to identify unequivocally any one type of coopetition as conducive to the achievement of better financial performance. One can only state that business groups with high cooperation and low competition scored better results in four out of six financial indicators analysed.

Different types of coopetition can be also distinguished based on the direction of cooperation and coopetition (see Chapter 2). In the study, two types of coopetition are distinguished: (1) unidirectional coopetition and (2) network coopetition. Unidirectional coopetition is pursued by nine business groups, while network coopetition by 112 business groups. Table 9.3 lists average values of the different financial indicators for both types of coopetition.

Unfortunately, again, the Mann-Whitney U test does not confirm the statistical significance of differences among business groups distinguished. However, comparison of average values of individual financial indicators enables certain conclusions to be drawn – for average values of all financial indicators tested are higher in business groups pursuing a network coopetition type than for those in which unidirectional coopetition prevails. Thus, one can cautiously assume that pursuing a network coopetition makes better financial performance possible compared to unidirectional coopetition. Coopetition among all companies, both vertical and horizontal, enables better financial performance.

Conclusion

The literature lacks publications directly tackling the relationship between an entity's coopetition and its financial performance. Most existing studies

Table 9.3 Coopetition types based on its direction versus financial performance of business groups studied

Variable	*Unidirectional coopetition*		*Network coopetition*	
	N[a]	*Average*	*N*[a]	*Average*
Gross profit [EUR]	8	39,121.23	83	65,409.50
EBIT Margin [%]	9	−1.04	102	2.97
Book value per share [EUR]	9	4.27	102	6.31
Operating revenue [EUR]	9	237,104.82	104	497,860.90
Net Income [EUR]	9	−2,184.04	104	22,927.55
Total assets [EUR]	9	142,652.38	104	844,541.58

Source: Own elaboration.
a Different N for each financial indicator due to no access to data.

focus on the inter-organisational coopetition and its impact on financial performance, but only few on the intra-organisational coopetition.

Based on the literature review, it is not possible to make a clear determination of the direction and strength of impact of coopetition (including intra-organisational coopetition) on financial performance. Although the prevailing view is that there exists a positive impact of coopetition (including intra-organisational coopetition) on financial performance. However, conclusions should be drawn carefully as methodological differences among studies are grate. In studies discussed, not only indicators use but also the number of indicators and definitions of financial performance variables differ. As a result, it can safely be said that the relationship between coopetition, including intra-organisational coopetition, on financial performance is underexplored.

To extend the knowledge on the relationship between coopetition and financial performance, the second section of this chapter discusses a study of business groups listed that pursue different types of intra-organisational coopetition.

The goal is to check whether the type of business groups' intra-organisational coopetition affects their financial performance and if so, then whether it is possible to identify which type of coopetition guarantees better financial performance for the business group pursuing it. The analysis of the results enables the following conclusions. First, increasing the intensity of cooperation in intra-organisational coopetition does not guarantee the improvement of all financial indicators considered of business groups analysed but only some. Business groups pursuing a high cooperation and low competition exhibit higher average values of four out of six financial indicators. The remaining two indicators turn out more favourable in business groups pursuing a coopetition characterised by a low intensity of both competition and cooperation. Unfortunately, the Mann-Whitney

U test does not confirm the existence of statistically significant differences between business groups. However, it can be stated that a high intensity of cooperation contributes to the improvement of only select financial indicators. Those observations could also be referred to conclusions of the study conducted by Liu et al. (2014), who analyse the impact of coopetition on financial performance. Their research shows that a higher intensity of coopetition positively influences companies' financial performance.

Second, average values for all six financial indicators analysed are higher for business groups implementing a network coopetition compared to business groups pursuing unidirectional coopetition. It is accordingly a warranted assertion that better financial performance is achieved by business groups opting for network coopetition, both vertical (with the parent company) and horizontal (subsidiaries among themselves), as compared to business groups with unidirectional coopetition. Unfortunately, the statistical testing does not yield itself to confirm the existence of statistically significant differences between two groups of entities distinguished based on the direction of coopetition.

In summary, the research conducted enables a cautious conclusion that the type of intra-organisational coopetition pursued by business groups may have impact on their financial performance. Coopetition with a high cooperation and low competition does not guarantee the improvement of all financial indicators but only some, while business groups pursuing network coopetition achieve better financial performance than groups pursuing unidirectional coopetition. The inference is, however, fraught with significant risk because the large disproportions in sizes of the samples, corresponding to specific types of intra-organisational coopetition, make impossible the statistical confirmation of the impact of the type of intra-organisational coopetition on financial performance. Considering the foregoing, the recommendation is to study a larger group of business groups selected with a view to this purpose and representing specific types of intra-organisational coopetition.

References

Bendig, D., Enke, S., Thieme, N. & Brettel, M. (2018). Performance implications of cross-functional coopetition in new product development: The mediating role of organizational learning. *Industrial Marketing Management*, 73, 137–153.

Bengtsson, M. & Raza-Ullah, T. (2016). A systematic review of research on coopetition: Toward a multilevel understanding. *Industrial Marketing Management*, 57, 23–39.

Crick, J.M. (2019). The dark side of coopetition: When collaborating with competitors is harmful for company performance. *Journal of Business & Industrial Marketing*, 35(2), 318–337.

Crick, J.M. & Crick, D. (2020). Coopetition and sales performance: Evidence from non-mainstream sporting clubs. *International Journal of Entrepreneurial Behavior & Research*, 27(9), 123–147.

Dorn, S., Schweiger, B. & Albers, S. (2016). Levels. phases and themes of coopetition: A systematic literature review and research agenda. *European Management Journal*, 34, 484–500.

Dubois, A. & Fredriksson, P. (2008). Cooperating and competing in supply networks: Making sense of a triadic sourcing strategy. *Journal of Purchasing and Supply Management*, 14(3), 170–179.

Gernsheimer, O., Kanbach, D.K. & Gast, J. (2021). Coopetition research - A systematic literature review on recent accomplishments and trajectories. *Industrial Marketing Management*, 96, 113–134.

Le Roy, F. & Sanou, F.H. (2014). Does coopetition strategy improve market performance? An empirical study in mobile phone industry. *Journal of Economics & Management*, 17, 64–92.

Liu, Y., Jiao, J. & Xia, J. (2019). Subsidiary networks and foreign subsidiary performance: A coopetition perspective. *Management and Organization Review*, 15(-1), 111–143.

Liu, Y., Luo, Y., Yang, P. & Maksimov, V. (2014). Typology and effects of coopetition in buyer-supplier relationships: Evidence from the Chinese home appliance industry. *Management and Organization Review*, 10(3), 439–465.

Luo, X., Slotegraaf, R.J. & Pan, X. (2006). Cross-functional "coopetition": The simultaneous role of cooperation and competition within firms. *Journal of Marketing*, 70(2), 67–80.

Morris, M.H., Kocak, A. & Ozer, A. (2007). Coopetition as a small business strategy: Implications for performance. *Journal of Small Business Strategy*, 18(1), 35–56.

Park, B.J. & Kim, D. (2020). Coopetition dynamics between giant entrants and incumbents in a new convergent segment: A case in the smartphone industry. *Asian Journal of Technology Innovation*, 29(3), 455–476.

Pekovic, S., Grolleau, G. & Mzoughi, N. (2020). Coopetition in innovation activities and firms' economic performance: An empirical analysis. *Creativity and Innovation Management*, 29(1), 85–98.

Peng, T-J.A., Pike, S., Chung-Hsin Yang, J. & Roos, G. (2012). Is cooperation with competitors a good idea? An example in practice. *British Journal of Management*, 23(4), 532–556.

Ritala, P. (2012). Coopetition strategy – when is it successful? Empirical evidence on innovation and market performance. *British Journal of Management*, 23(3), 307–324.

Robert, F., Marques, P. & Le Roy, F. (2009). Coopetition between SMEs: An empirical study of French professional football. *International Journal of Entrepreneurship and Small Business*, 8(1), 23–43.

Sanou, F.H., Le Roy, F. & Gnyawali, D.R. (2016). How does centrality in coopetition networks matter? An empirical investigation in the mobile telephone industry. *British Journal of Management*, 27(1), 143–160.

Wemmer, F., Emrich, E. & Koenigstorfer, J. (2016). The impact of coopetition-based open innovation on performance in nonprofit sports clubs. *European Sport Management Quarterly*, 16(3), 341–363.

10 Managing Coopetition within a Business Group

Wioletta Mierzejewska and Patryk Dziurski

Introduction

The book provides a framework for better understanding coopetition within business groups by explaining the essence of coopetition therein, its modes, determinants, and outcomes as it is a relevant and important topic. The various aspects discussed in the book give interesting insights into relationships among entities in complex organisations, such as a business group. Coopetition within business groups is accounted as an intra-organisational coopetition, which is a largely uncharted territory as researchers focus mainly on coopetition among organisationally and legally independent parties. However, simultaneous cooperation and competition relationships can be also found on each level of an organisation as it occurs between individual employees, project teams, departments, units, among others. In the long lifecycles of a business group, cooperation as well as competition emerge among subsidiaries therein. Thus, this chapter shows the generic model of coopetition within a business group based on the theoretical and empirical conclusions presented in the book. The model is useful for researchers as it summarises findings on coopetition within a business group and is a roadmap for further research. It is also interesting for managers as it shows the strategic perspective of coopetition within business groups. The chapter also summarises findings from the empirical research presented in book, includes theoretical and practical implications of the study, and proposes direction for further research.

Strategic Coopetition within Business Groups

Business groups are complex organisations that are often characterised by complex ownership structures. Chapter 1 shows that they are distinguished from other network organisations, but there is still no single, commonly approved definition of a business group. However, there are two commonly used approaches to define a business group: sociology- and economics-based (Cuervo-Cazurra, 2006; Aluchna, 2010). The former defines a business group via formal and informal ties among subsidiarise, while the latter, followed by the book, is narrower and focuses on equity ties.

DOI: 10.4324/9781003324775-11

Business groups operate in both developing and developed economies. They function in different economic conditions that result in high diversity of business groups. Previous studies explain the existence of business groups with the use of some main theoretical approach, such as market imperfection (institutional void), cultural heritage (relational perspective), and political economy. However, one can also encounter explanations rooted in the agency theory, resource-based theory, and theory of firm growth. As far as Polish business groups are concerned, one can identify two main logics of their origin. The first one is the privatisation and commercialisation of complex state-owned entities into business groups. The second one is the growth of private companies that have transformed into business groups for many different reasons (Romanowska, 1998). At present, according to Statistics Poland, there is a trend for the growing importance of business groups and their role in the Polish economy. It is manifested through the economic strength of business groups, their profitability, role as important employers, and activity on foreign markets (Enterprise groups in Poland in 2020, 2022).

Coopetition in business groups translates into simultaneous cooperation and competition among subsidiaries (Luo, 2005; Hong & Snell, 2015; Tippmann et al., 2018). Chapter 2 shows that cooperation and competition differ due to intensity in business groups surveyed. The main relationship between subsidiaries is high-intensity cooperation with low-intensity competition. Thus, in business groups surveyed, cooperation-dominated coopetition prevails. This finding is consistent with the nature of a business group wherein individual subsidiaries cooperate to achieve goals set by the parent company. It may also show the significant cohesion of business groups studied but also the strong influence of the parent company on internal relationships within the group. This observation and following ones prove the distinct nature of coopetition in business groups from one between legally independent firms. Interestingly, in business groups studied, coopetition usually manifests itself in the areas of finance, sales, procurement, and production. This can be due to the joint pursuit of various projects and a group structure that focuses on production processes, supply, and sales, but also competition for internal financing or product competition on the external market. Thus, coopetition areas in business groups studied cover primary and support activities of a value chain. Additionally, in business groups studied, simultaneous vertical and horizontal cooperation as well as competition prevail. It is found, considering areas and direction of coopetition, that business groups studied predominately follow the complex network coopetition – horizontal and vertical network competition and cooperation across multiple areas of a value chain. This reinforces the view of a business group as network featuring a diversity of relationships among subsidiaries (Carney et al., 2011).

Coopetition with its equally important interrelated contradictory logics is a paradoxical relationship capable of creating instability and tensions.

Ambidextrous managers may be required to manage tensions in this relationship. For this reason, previous studies discuss what skillsets could make managers ambidextrous (Czakon et al., 2020). Scholars argue that organisations need capable managers with skills to manage both exploration and exploitation; however, not only the nature of managers' skillsets is important but also their direct relationship with coopetition itself (Fernandez et al., 2014; Bengtsson et al., 2016; Czakon et al., 2020). Results presented in Chapter 3 suggest that majority of managers (in their own opinion) possess ambidextrous skills of simultaneous cooperation and competition when engaging in a coopetition relationship. The study also shows that managers surveyed, facing a crisis, are predisposed to cooperation. Behaviours toward cooperation are exhibited more often than behaviours toward competition. Tensions arising in coopetition relationships may be either interpersonally or substantively. In most business groups studied, substantive conflicts are observed more often than interpersonal ones. The fact of belonging to a business group indisputably has an impact on attitudes and behaviours of managers both in the parent company and subsidiaries determining their engagement in cooperation and competition, perception of tensions (conflicts), and ways of dealing with them.

Coopetition within business groups, similar to inter-organisational one, is determined by multiple factors that are related to the environment and a business group's characteristics. In the study, based on the factor analysis, main factors determining coopetition in a business group are identified. Chapter 4 shows that the most important external factors are globalisation, technological development, as well as industry innovation, internationalisation, and maturity. This is consistent with other studies demonstrating the importance of the technological, social, or political uncertainty of the environment as a factor stimulating the emergence of simultaneous cooperation and competition among different entities (Chambers, 2015). Among internal factors, the most important ones are unit independence, group complexity, centralisation of activities, allocation of resources to subsidiaries, size and age of a business group, its strategy, and characteristics of its shareholders. It means that coopetition in business groups is driven by internal organisation and strategy that confirm other studies (Li et al., 2007; Chambers, 2015). It is also often resource-driven coopetition, especially where resource allocation to subsidiaries is inadequate leaving them with unfulfilled investment needs.

The important topic in intra-organisational coopetition in business group's studies is the allocation of resources to subsidiaries. Existing research demonstrates that a shortage of resources needed to pursue entities' strategic goals leads to competition for resources from the parent company, but it may be also a reason for cooperation among subsidiaries to share limited resources (Li et al., 2009; Maurer, 2011; Chambers, 2015). Key resource characteristics are rarity, difficulty of imitation or substitution, and importance to value creation. Resources with different characteristics being in a possession of a subsidiary impact its and other behaviours in a business group and, therefore, show different propensity to competition and cooperation. Simultaneously, due to limited freedom of subsidiaries' decision-making, they may be forced by the parent company to share resources meaning that subsidiaries with resources of strategic value may lose competitive advantage. Chapter 5 investigates the relationship between allocation of resources to subsidiaries in business groups and coopetition type. Unfortunately, results of empirical studies do not confirm the relationship assessed. It seems that only a weak relationship exists between coopetition types identify based on the direction of cooperation and competition and allocation of resources to subsidiaries. In all other cases, no statistically significant correlation is identified. On the one hand, it may be the consequence of the sufficient resource allocation in business groups studied, but on the other hand, it may be linked with overoptimistic view on resource allocation of respondents from the parent company.

Internationalisation of business groups is another interesting topic discussed in the book in the context of coopetition relations. Research on inter-organisational coopetition proves the interdependence between coopetition and internationalisation of a company (Jankowska, 2011) as coopetition is a factor that promotes and facilitates internationalisation (Monticelli et al., 2018). In the case of coopetition in complex entities, it is most often described on the example of multinational enterprises (Luo, 2005). Chapter 6 shows that international business groups more often than domestic ones exhibit simultaneous cooperative and competitive behaviours. Subsidiaries in international business groups compete for parent company's investments, but also in the case of similar scopes of activities, they compete on external market. This study carefully confirms that network coopetition and high cooperation going together with low competition coexists with international scope of operations of business groups studied. It is argued that for international business group's cooperation is needed to fulfil goals, and competition is emerging (however to small extend) as an effect of efficiency rivalry.

Chapter 7 focuses on coopetition and corporate governance within business groups showing increasing interest in corporate governance in complex organisations (Ahmed & Uddin, 2018; Sanan et al., 2021). Features of a business group make the nature and focus of corporate governance different compared to standalone firms (Hsieh et al., 2010), thus also impacting coopetition in business groups. Results of the empirical studies confirm the existence of relationship between the intensity of intra-organisational coopetition within business groups and selected features of corporate governance therein. It is shown that the concentration of control and presence of an industry investor as the dominant shareholder are negatively associated with the intensity of coopetition, while the interlocking directorates policy and investment role of the parent company are positively linked with the intensity of coopetition. Additionally, results of the studies do not confirm the existence of the relationship between adoption of universal procedures at the group level and the intensity of intra-group coopetition. Results suggest that corporate governance may either foster, hamper or be neutral to coopetition in business groups, thus managers should consider corporate governance mechanism to impact coopetition.

Coopetition within business groups emerges in high-, medium-, and low-tech industries; however, technological intensity of an industry in which business group operates impacts the intensity of cooperation, competition, and direction of coopetition (Cygler, 2009; Gnyawali & Park, 2011). Chapter 8 sheds lights on the prevalent coopetition type implemented by business groups in high-, medium-, and low-tech industries and verifies if the technological intensity of an industry impacts type of coopetition within a business group. The study does not allow to identify which coopetition type is prevailed in high-, medium-, and low-tech industries, but it does show that business groups in high-tech industries experience higher competition intensity than business groups in medium- and low-tech industries. Thus, the study does not confirm the relationship between technological intensity of an industry and coopetition type, but it confirms the existence of the relationship between technological intensity of an industry and competition intensity within business groups studied. Results show that features of high-tech industries, especially high internal and external competitive pressure that could be caused by high-technological advancement of an industry, intensify competition among entities within a business group.

Several studies that focus on coopetition highlight benefits of it, and some research demonstrates the positive impact of coopetition on firms' performance even taking the related hazards into account (Peng et al. 2012; Dorn et al., 2016; Crick, 2019; Liu et al., 2019). For intra-organisational coopetition, a low intensity of competition combined with cooperation may generate positive financial results for the whole business group. This is because intra-organisational competition may serve as a catalyst for improved performance of subsidiaries that are evaluated by the parent company. Unfortunately, empirical studies presented in Chapter 9 do not confirm statistically the existence of the relationship between coopetition types and financial performance of business groups studied. Conducted analyses show that business groups pursuing network coopetition achieve better financial results than business groups with unidirectional coopetition. At the same time, coopetition with high level of cooperation does not guarantee the improvement of all financial indicators, but only some of them.

Generic Model of Coopetition within a Business Group

Prior studies have focuses mainly on the coopetition between legally and organisationally independent firms but often neglected coopetition within business groups (Bouncken et al., 2015; Bengtsson & Raza-Ullah, 2016; Gernsheimer et al., 2021). It does not allow to understand the concept of coopetition completely as business groups significantly differs from standalone firms. Business group represents specific organisational model between hierarchies and markets as coopeting entities within a business group are linked by equity and social ties, and they are not independent in their strategic choices. They may intensively cooperate and occasionally compete, but in other circumstances, competition may prevail, while cooperation may be rare or both relationships may be balanced. Additionally, control and incentives mechanisms implemented by the parent company as well as structure and type of ties between entities may enhance or hamper both internal cooperation and competition. Thus, coopetition within business groups is exceptional and shedding light on internal relations in business groups is interesting for coopetition studies, especially that drivers, areas, as well as outcomes of coopetition within business groups differ from those between independent firms.

Coopetition within a business group can be described by the intensity of cooperation and competition between entities therein, and by areas and direction of competition and cooperation. Thus, managers in business groups should focus on intensity, areas, and direction of both relationships to achieve the best outcome. To explain the complexity of coopetition within a business group, based on the findings presented in the book, authors developed the generic model that is shown in Figure 10.1.

Coopetition in business group is a process combining cooperation and competition that emerges vertically and horizontally between some or all entities. The dominant behaviour of entities towards others (both sister companies and the parent company) creates the internal coopetitive environment. Therefore, coopetition could be cooperation-dominated, competition-dominated, and balanced as entities in a business group express cooperative and competitive behaviours of varying intensity. However, the

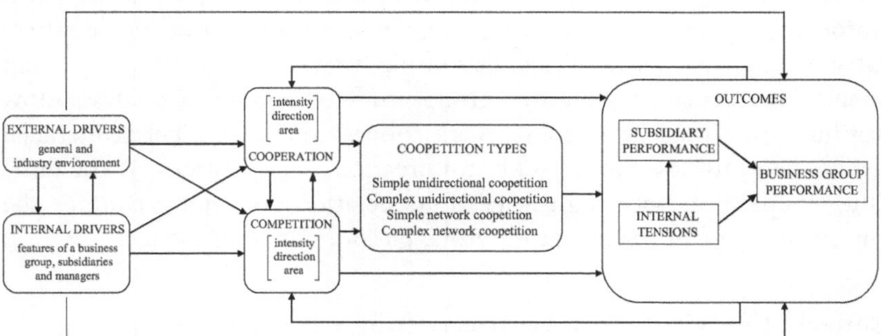

Figure 10.1 Generic model of coopetition within a business group.
Source: Own elaboration.

comprehensive evaluation of relations in business groups leads to a conclusion that cooperation-dominated coopetition prevails. It is due to organisation model of a business group, common goals, as well as coordination mechanisms implemented by the parent company to control, exploit cooperation, and prevent excessive competition that could be destructive.

Simultaneous cooperation and competition in a business group emerge vertically and horizontally and they cover primary and support activities of a value chain. However, cooperation can be found most often in vertical relationships in all areas of a value chain, while competition occurs in horizontal relationships, and it covers mainly rivalry for resources and position in a business group. Considering areas and directions of cooperation and competition, four types of coopetition within a business group can be distinguished:

- simple unidirectional coopetition that emerges horizontally or vertically and covers small number of areas of a value chain,
- complex unidirectional coopetition that emerges horizontally or vertically and covers large number of areas of a value chain,
- simple network coopetition that emerges horizontally and vertically and covers small number of areas of value a chain,
- complex network coopetition that emerges horizontally and vertically and covers large number of areas of a value chain.

The most common coopetition type in business groups is complex network coopetition. It is due to the network nature of a business group in which entities are linked by multiple formal and informal relationships. The second common type of coopetition that can be found in business groups is simple network coopetition. It characterises more loose business groups in which entities cooperate and compete but not so intensively and not in many areas. The last two types, i.e. simple as well as complex unidirectional coopetition, emerge rarely in business groups.

Cooperation and competition are driven by external and internal factors. External factors that influence cooperation and competition relationships, and thus coopetition type, relate to the industry and general environment. Business groups operating in hypercompetitive, globalised, and technological advanced environment represent more intensive cooperation and competition that cover multiple areas. However, internal factors of coopetition prevail in business groups. Those factors relate to features of a business group, subsidiaries, and managers whose ambitions influence internal relations and can enhance rivalry for power and position within a group. Managers may be more or less oriented toward cooperation or competition and thus take more cooperative or competitive attitude toward other entities in a business group. Internal cooperation and competition are also determined by location, resource endowment, size, as well as scope of activity of subsidiaries. Domain overlap and lack of resources to gain expected goals may by a driving mechanism for subsidiaries to pursue more competitive behaviours in a business group, whereas cooperation can be related to operational, technological, or strategical interdependence of subsidiaries. Coopetition is largely determined by business group organisation and its strategy as well. Business group organisation model may favour or restrain cooperation and competition. Coherent business groups with subsidiaries supporting the parent company exhibit more intensive cooperation than competition. In business groups, acting as loose federation with shallow and weak ties between entities, competition relationships can occur more often. Business group organisational design is closely related to the implemented strategy. The greater level of diversification and the multinational strategy favour more intense competition in many fields, while the transnational strategy with high interdependence of subsidiaries is associated with greater cooperation.

Coopetition in business groups generates positive as well as negative outcomes. Positive outcomes relate to subsidiaries and the whole business group performance. According to previous studies, coopetition in business group enhance innovation, strategic, and financial performance (Luo, 2005; Tippmann et al., 2018; Liu et al., 2019). Cooperation with small extent of competition positively impacts subsidiaries' efficiency. However, internal competition is accompanied by tensions, conflicts, and asymmetry of interests. Coopetition in business group with too intense competition leads to value destruction. Thus, managers in business groups should crucially monitor and, sometimes, even stimulate cooperative and competitive behaviours of subsidiaries but simultaneously not allow to excessive competition that leads to performance decrease.

Theoretical and Practical Implications

Findings from the study presented in the book allow to formulate several implications for theory and business practice. First, the book enriches studies on business groups that are common organisational form across the world. They consist of legally independent firms linked by ownership, economic, and social ties (Cuervo-Cazurra, 2006, 2018). Business group's research focuses mainly on definition, justification, or performance of subsidiaries and the whole business group, but only some deal with internal mechanisms and relations therein (Yiu et al., 2007). Moreover, relationships in business groups are most often analysed from the perspective of cooperation theory. This book allows to better understand internal relationships within a business group using coopetition lenses. Additionally, the book also gives an insight into issues of business group functioning like internationalisation, subsidiaries resource endowment, financial performance, and so on. Second, the book broaden knowledge on coopetition. Empirical studies confirm that entities in business groups not only cooperate, but they also compete. Thus, the book contributes to the coopetition research by exploring intra-organisational level of coopetitive behaviours. Previous studies on coopetition focus mostly on inter-organisational level, and those on intra-organisational level are mainly theoretical or qualitative (Li et al., 2009; Chiambaretto et al., 2019; Gernsheimer et al., 2021). The research presented in this book explore intra-organisational coopetition in quantitative manner and from the perspective of the parent company. It is a complementary perspective as earlier studies explore coopetition in complex organisation from the perspective of individual entity (Luo, 2005; Liu et al., 2019). It is argued that the perspective of the parent company is important as it controls and coordinates subsidiaries and heavily influences cooperation and competition relationships in a business group. Third, this book proves that coopetition at each organisational level differs due to scope, drivers, and outcomes. It enriches coopetition studies by underlining the diversity and complexity of coopetitive relationship. Fourth, the important theoretical contribution of this book is a generic model of coopetition within a business group as it combines business group research stream with the literature on coopetition. Both phenomena – business groups and coopetition – are of a great importance in many economies and organisations; therefore, combining them in one study allows for better understanding of simultaneous cooperation and competition in complex organisations prevailing in many countries around the world. Generic model of coopetition within a business group describes intra-group coopetition in comprehensive manner with the emphasis on its types, drivers, and outcomes. Proposed model is a theoretical model that results from both conceptual and empirical studies presented in the book and sheds light onto coopetitive behaviours in business groups.

This book provides practical implications too. It highlights the importance of the awareness of managers of coopetition within a business group. Cooperation is more natural and prevailed relationship in a business group, but competition also occurs. Lack of managers' awareness of those contradictory relationships may negatively impact business group's performance. Hence, managers in business groups should control and coordinate cooperation and competition that arise inside. Cooperation is needed to gain synergy, competition is, however, beneficial too. Healthy competition enhances efficiency of subsidiaries, but too much competition may be destructive (Luo, 2005).

This book also highlights importance of different factors that drive coopetition in business groups. Managers should take into consideration not only external factors emerging from the general environment and industry in which a business group operates in, but more importantly, internal factors related mainly to organisation of a business group, its strategy, and resources endowment. Managers, making decision on the strategy executed, organisational design implemented, and resource endowment, may either foster or hamper cooperation and competition and, therefore, coopetition in a business group.

Coopetition management in a business group should be aimed at monitoring cooperation and competition, shaping internal environment, introducing internal coordination mechanisms and incentive systems, as well as managing tensions and conflicts occurring naturally in a coopetition relationship. Management of coopetition is an extremely difficult task for managers, especially giving different goals and ambitions of managers of subsidiaries therein.

Further Research Directions

The book combines two research domains – coopetition and business group – to stimulate research in both. Coopetition within a business group is under researched topic that is worth further and deeper analysis. Insights provided in the book help to explore coopetition within a business group, but still some aspects of it remain insufficiently recognised.

The study investigates coopetition within a business group from the perspective of the parent company neglecting the perspective of subsidiaries. Therefore, network analyses involving the perspective of all parties in a business group should be incorporated in future studies as it will allow to gain better understanding of coopetition in complex organisations. Moreover, generic model of coopetition in a business group proposed should be verified in empirical studies. It is developed based on separated research results and literature analysis presented in the book, thus it is worth to assess it in more advanced research. Additionally, future studies should focus more on coopetition management in a business group as it will provide more detailed recommendations for managers and, therefore, allow them to benefit more from coopetition and limit its downsides. Effective coopetition management seems to be crucial to not only to survive but mainly to thrive.

References

Ahmed, S. & Uddin, S. (2018). Toward a political economy of corporate governance change and stability in family business groups: A morphogenetic approach. *Accounting, Auditing & Accountability Journal*, 31(8), 2192–2217.

Aluchna, M. (2010), *Kierunki rozwoju polskich grup kapitałowych: Perspektywa międzynarodowa* [Directions of growth of Polish business groups: International perspective]. Warszawa: Oficyna Wydawnicza SGH.

Bengtsson, M. & Raza-Ullah, T. (2016). A systematic review of research on coopetition: Toward a multilevel understanding. *Industrial Marketing Management*, 57, 23–39.

Bengtsson, M., Raza-Ullah, T. & Vanyushyn, V. (2016). The coopetition paradox and tension: The moderating role of coopetition capability. *Industrial Marketing Management*, 53, 19–30.

Bouncken, R.B., Gast, J., Kraus, S. & Bogers, M. (2015). Coopetition: A systematic review, synthesis, and future research directions. *Review of Managerial Science*, 9(3), 577–601.

Chambers, M. (2015). *Dynamic inter-subsidiary relationships of competition and collaboration*. Dissertation. Cranfield University.

Carney, M., Gedajlovic, E.R., Heugens, P.P., Van Essen, M. & Van Oosterhout, J. (2011). Business group affiliation, performance, context, and strategy: A meta-analysis. *Academy of Management Journal*, 54(3), 437–460.

Chiambaretto, P., Massé, D. & Mirc, N. (2019). "All for One and One for All?" Knowledge broker roles in managing tensions of internal coopetition: The Ubisoft case. *Research Policy*, 48(3), 584–600.

Crick, J.M. (2019). The dark side of coopetition: When collaborating with competitors is harmful for company performance. *Journal of Business & Industrial Marketing*, 35(2), 318–337.

Cygler, J. (2009). *Kooperencja przedsiębiorstw. Czynniki sektorowe i korporacyjne* [Firms coopetition. Industry-related and corporate factors]. Warszawa: Oficyn Wydawnicza SGH.

Cuervo-Cazurra, A. (2006). Business groups and their types. *Asia Pacific Journal of Management*, 23(4), 419–437.

Cuervo-Cazurra, A. (2018). The evolution of business groups' corporate social responsibility. *Journal of Business Ethics*, 153(4), 997–1016.

Czakon, W., Klimas, P., & Mariani, M. (2020). Behavioral antecedents of coopetition: A synthesis and measurement scale. *Long Range Planning*, 53(1), 101875.

Czakon, W., Srivastava, M.K., Le Roy, F. & Gnyawali, D. (2020). Coopetition strategies: Critical issues and research directions. *Long Range Planning*, 53(1), 101948.

Dorn, S., Schweiger, B. & Albers, S. (2016). Levels. phases and themes of coopetition: A systematic literature review and research agenda. *European Management Journal*, 34, 484–500.

Enterprise groups in Poland in 2020 (2022). Report of Statistics Poland, Poland.

Fernandez, A.S., Ji, F.X. & Yami, S. (2014). Balancing exploration and exploitation tension in coopetition: The case of European space innovation programmes. *International Journal of Business Environment*, 6(1), 69–91.

Gernsheimer, O., Kanbach, D.K. & Gast, J. (2021). Coopetition research - A systematic literature review on recent accomplishments and trajectories. *Industrial Marketing Management*, 96, 113–134.

Gnyawali, D.R. & Park, B-J. (2011). Co-opetition between giants: Collaboration with competitors for technological innovation. *Research Policy*, 40(5), 650–663.

Hong, J.F. & Snell, R.S. (2015). Knowledge development through co-opetition: A case study of a Japanese foreign subsidiary and its local suppliers. *Journal of World Business*, 50(4), 769–780.

Hsieh, T.-J., Yeh, R.S. & Chen, Y.-J. (2010). Business groups characteristics and affiliated from innovation: The case of Taiwan. *Industrial Marketing Management*, 39, 560–576.

Jankowska, B. (2011). Implications of coopetition for international competitiveness and internationalization of firms: Perspective of SME and large companies. *International Journal of Business and Management Studies*, 3(1), 49–58.

Li, D., Ferreira, M.P. & Serra, F.R. (2007). *Technology transfer within MNEs: An investigation of inter-subsidiary competition and cooperation*. ADVANTAGE Working Paper, No.1, Instituto Politécnicode Leiria, Leiria.

Li, D., Ferreira, M.P. & Serra F.R. (2009). Technology transfer within MNEs: Inter-subsidiary competition and cooperation. *RAI-Revista de Administração e Inovação*, 6(1), 139–158.

Liu, Y., Jiao, J. & Xia, J. (2019). Subsidiary networks and foreign subsidiary performance: A coopetition perspective. *Management and Organization Review*, 15(1), 111–143.

Luo, Y. (2005). Toward coopetition within a multinational enterprise: A perspective from foreign subsidiaries. *Journal of World Business*, 40(1), 71–90.

Maurer, J. (2011). *Relationships between foreign subsidiaries: Competition and cooperation in multinational plant engineering companies*. Wiesbaden: Springer Science & Business Media.

Monticelli, J.M., Garrido, I.L. & de Vasconcellos, S.L. (2018). Coopetition and institutions: A strategy for Brazilian wineries facing internationalization. *International Journal of Wine Business Research*, 30(1), 74–95.

Peng, T-J.A., Pike, S., Chung-Hsin Yang, J. & Roos, G. (2012). Is cooperation with competitors a good idea? An example in practice. *British Journal of Management*, 23(4), 532–556.

Romanowska, M. (1998). Strategie grup kapitałowych w Polsce [Strategies of business groups in Poland], in Romanowska, M., Trocki, M. & Wawrzyniak, B. (eds) *Grupy kapitałowe w Polsce* [Business groups in Polnad]. Warszawa: Difin.

Sanan, N.K., Jaisinghani, D. & Yadav, S. (2019). Corporate governance, firm performance, and business group affiliation: Evidence from India. *Management Decision*, 58(8), 1863–1876.

Tippmann, E., Scott, P.S., Reilly, M. & O'Brien, D. (2018). Subsidiary coopetition competence: Navigating subsidiary evolution in the multinational corporation. *Journal of World Business*, 53(4), 540–554.

Yiu, D.W., Lu, Y., Bruton, G.D. & Hoskisson, R.E. (2007). Business groups: An integrated model to focus future research. *Journal of Management Studies*, 44(8), 1551–1579.

Index

Note: **Bold** page numbers refer to tables; *italic* page numbers refer to figures and page numbers followed by "n" denote endnotes.